SERIGRAPHY

SILK SCREEN TECHNIQUES FOR THE ARTIST

KENNETH W. AUVIL
Associate Professor of Art, San Jose State College

PRENTICE-HALL, INC., Englewood Cliffs, New Jersey

PRENTICE-HALL INTERNATIONAL, INC., *London*
PRENTICE-HALL OF AUSTRALIA, PTY., LTD., *Sydney*
PRENTICE-HALL OF CANADA, LTD., *Toronto*
PRENTICE-HALL OF INDIA (PRIVATE) LTD., *New Delhi*
PRENTICE-HALL OF JAPAN, INC., *Tokyo*

Current printing (last digit):

11   10   9   8   7   6   5   4   3

Library of Congress Catalog Card Number: 65-16337

Printed in the United States of America: 80716-C

PREFACE

During the last few decades the printmaker has discovered a great diversity of methods for developing and duplicating image form. All of the major printing processes have undergone startling transformations due to new materials and techniques and to the artist's insistent search for fresh visual stimuli. The silk screen process, a youngster among the fine art print media, has an ardent group of followers who favor the flexibility the screen provides in color, and value the unique characteristics of the stencil-derived image. Other factors contribute to the interest in screen printing: the basic techniques are easily and rapidly acquired; the equipment is simple, portable, and inexpensive; the artist may work in large or small sizes with equal ease, develop his image spontaneously or deliberately, and exploit opaque or transparent color in a vast range of textural and linear configurations. The screen is one of the most autographic of the print media; during the evolution of the image, a close, direct association is maintained with preceding stages of development, and the image on the screen does not reverse, left to right, when printed.

The silk screen prints reproduced in this book should illustrate the variety of image form possible in the screen. The text defines the operations and materials that influence the development of the image, and describes the methods most frequently used to make original screen prints.

The first chapters deal with the screen and related equipment that should be acquired or constructed for work in the medium. The next chapters present methods of image formulation with the screen and describe the resources and techniques the artist may use in stencil making, color mixing, and printing. The final chapters cover the disposition of the finished print, its processing and presentation.

For those who are unfamiliar with the medium, specific working methods are thoroughly detailed to eliminate many minor, but irritating, technical problems. The beginner should be able to find a comfortable working association with the screen without needless frustration.

ACKNOWLEDGMENTS

Glen Alps, artist and professor at the University of Washington, first introduced the silk screen medium to me; his instruction was a valuable stimulus to my early interest in printmaking and he has been a source of encouragement in the years of our friendship since that time. My own students should receive credit for motivating the sheaf of instruction sheets that became the nucleus for this book, and for generating problems to be explored and clarified in the text. My wife, Mary, edited the manuscript, photographed and processed all but a few of the illustrations, with great skill throughout. I am grateful to the artists included here for their interest, cooperation, and prompt response, and to Edward Thomas and the Seattle Art Museum staff for their aid in acquiring photographs of the Japanese stencils. Marian Britton of the Original Prints Gallery and Dennis Beall of the Achenbach Foundation have contributed needed information.

Some of the technical data was supplied by business firms. Ted Leber of the Ralph Leber Company has given me much advice on printing inks. The Sherwin-Williams Company, the American Screen Process Equipment Company, and Western Sign Supply, Inc., have also fulfilled my requests.

CONTENTS

SERIGRAPHY
Silk Screen Techniques for the Artist

1
THE MEDIUM

Serigraphy is the artist's term for his use of the silk screen process, which is a special adaption of a very old method of duplicating an image, printing by stencil. Stencils in their simplest form are made from thin, durable materials, such as paper, plastic, or metal, from which a figure or shape is cut. The stencil is placed on a surface, covering it except for the area exposed through the opening in the stencil material. Paint can then be mopped over the exposed surface, and when the stencil is removed an exact image of the open area remains on the surface in paint. The stencil can be moved to a fresh surface and the operation repeated, each time exactly duplicating the shape of the stencil opening. The stencil material serves as a protective mask to prevent paint from contacting any part not exposed through the opening.

Night Landscape by Glen Alps

1

FIG. 1–1
The simple stencil

With some variation of materials, the simple stencil has been used for centuries to apply decorative forms to textiles, wallpaper, furniture, and many other items. Early woodcut illustrations were sometimes enriched with stencilled colors; today everyone is familiar with the stencil lettering on packages and crates.

FIG. 1–2
Japanese paper stencil, 18–19th century (Eugene Fuller Memorial Collection, Seattle Art Museum)

To make the simple stencil self-supporting, elements often must be included in the stencil which may require compromises in image design. Slender peninsulas or detached areas can easily be displaced or damaged by the printing tool; such areas must be secured to firmer parts of the stencil through bridges or ties. The ties, of course, appear on the printed image and may become intruding elements in the desired impression.

To overcome this limitation, centuries ago Japanese stencil makers began supporting complex stencil parts with threads of silk or hair. These artists became so adept that they could print stencils which were unbelievably intricate (Fig. 1–2). The stencils were cut from thin waterproofed paper, and the supporting strands were so fine that their impression did not show when the stencil was printed.

The thread ties of the Japanese stencil were often attached in a regular pattern of such close grouping as to suggest a woven mesh (Fig. 1–3) and may well have inspired the use of silk cloth as a

FIG. 1–3
Japanese paper stencil (detail) (Eugene Fuller Memorial Collection, Seattle Art Museum)

stencil support. With a weave open enough to allow paint to pass through easily, but made of strands so fine they leave no prominent impression, silk cloth is an ideal material for printing the stencil image and provides a durable, stable base for making and retaining accurate positioning of the stencil parts.

The use of a screen with silk cloth as the stencil carrier was developed in Europe about the beginning of this century. Silk screen equipment has been refined but not essentially changed since that time. The screen of today consists of a simple rigid frame on which the fabric is stretched drum tight. The stencil is attached to the underside of the fabric or imbedded directly in the mesh. The stencil is printed in the same manner as the simple stencil; the paint is applied through the top side of the screen and forced through the mesh and open areas of the stencil onto the surface below.

The standard tool for applying paint through the simple stencil is the brush. The brush is used sometimes in silk screen printing as well, especially in Japan. However, in western countries the most common device for manipulating the paint mixture on the screen is a flexible blade fixed in a handle. This tool, the "squeegee," rapidly spreads a thin, even coat of paint over the screen. One stroke deposits paint through all of the open areas of the stencil onto the surface below.

FIG. 1–4
The silk screen

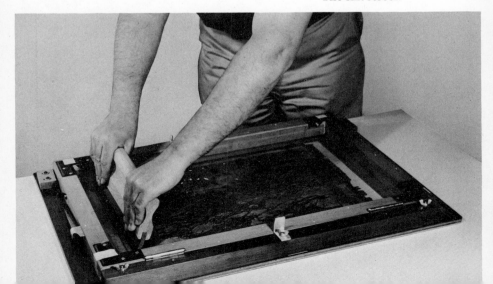

With each stroke of the squeegee, one copy is printed in one color. If additional colors are to be used, a separate stencil must be made for each. All the copies are first printed in one color. The stencil is then changed and each copy is again printed in the second color. A register system is employed to align the second color, and all those following, to the first printing. Each color is printed in turn on all copies before the next color is applied.

These are the fundamentals of screen printing, a process not unlike simple stencil printing in principle, but offering far more flexibility in the development of image form. With the stable stencil carrier a greater range of stencil materials and techniques can be employed and a precise system of registration can be established to assure accurate color alignment. The equipment for color printing, even of large prints, is simple and inexpensive and the technique is quickly mastered.

The commercial printer found a bonanza in the silk screen process; surprisingly the medium did not become known and practiced by the artist as an expressive means until it had been used commercially in this country for about thirty years. Partly responsible was the mysterious secrecy with which the commercial shops enveloped their discovery. However, fine art printmaking in all media suffered neglect until the 1930's when artists began a vast exploration and experimentation in all the fine art print processes. The time was ripe for the silk screen to be examined for its potential.

At this time a group of artists, headed by Anthony Velonis, applied and received permission to set up a WPA program to investigate the silk screen as a fine art medium. The screen was used, not for reproduction, but for the creation of original works of art. Upon this initial impetus, supported by early adherents such as Guy Maccoy, Edward Landon, Harry Gottlieb, Elizabeth McCausland, and many other artists and critics, the growth of the medium as a fine art tool was explosive. In its brief existence, the fine art silk screen has taken its place with the older printmaking processes as a major expressive means. The number of artists working in the screen medium continues to grow, and through their individual explorations the flexibility of the medium continues to expand.

Soon after its initiation the fine art screen print was given the name *serigraph* by the WPA group and Carl Zigrosser, Curator of

Prints at the Philadelphia Museum of Art. The term is universally used today to distinguish the original screen print from a commercial reproduction, which retains the name, *silk screen process print*.

The implication of the label *serigraph* has greater significance than just an attempt to apply an exclusive title to the medium as used by the artist. The printing methods used in serigraphy and in screen process printing are similar, but the intent differs. The silk screen medium, like other media, leaves its characteristic imprint on the image form. These characteristics are sought by the artist to implement his graphic presentation. Those forms derived from experience unique with a medium are much valued by the artist, and become part of his total complex of expressive means. When the screen process is used for commercial reproduction, such as of an oil painting or watercolor, there is no intent to utilize the inherent visual characteristics produced by the medium. The aim is to reproduce, through the silk screen process, a form already completed, almost always in some other medium. On the other hand, the serigrapher uses the screen as a primary means of developing his image, a first-hand expressive tool.

Efforts have been made to clarify the distinction between a reproduction and an original print, notably by the Print Council of America. In their booklet, *What is an Original Print?*,* they have proposed the following criteria:

> An original print is a work of art, the general requirements of which are:
> 1. The artist alone has created the master image in or upon the plate, stone, wood block or other material, for the purpose of creating the print.
> 2. The print is made directly from the said material, by the artist or pursuant to his directions.
> 3. The finished print is approved by the artist.

Usually the term *print* also implies *print edition,* or a duplication of the impression. The precision of duplication is controlled by the artist, and variance in the image form from copy to copy is tolerated if, upon inspection by the artist, the printed image passes his qualifi-

---

* Joshua Binion Cahn, ed., *What is an Original Print?* (New York: Print Council of America, 1964), p. 9.

cations for his expressive intent. Usually he will strive to maintain consistency in what he considers the best presentation state of his idea. A proof with a notable variation from the general appearance of the bulk of the edition would not be included in the edition. If the proof is a choice piece, as good or better than the edition copies, it is still a print, but an independent, unique copy. It may be valued equally with, but not included in, the edition.

Duplication, as the reader may have guessed, is not the sole reason for using the silk screen medium, and probably for most serigraphers not even a primary reason. However, the limitations on expressive form imposed by the diciplines required for tolerable image duplication are not forbidding restrictions that hinder a fluid handling of image form. On the contrary, the diciplines demanded for duplication control may have quite the opposite effect of revealing and expanding the possible ways of visually expressing an idea. The qualities unique to the screen are reason enough for including the medium in the artist's tools for making a graphic statement. With familiarity, the characteristics of a medium become a manner of speaking, a dialect of visual presentation, comfortable and expressive to the individual.

2
EQUIPPING THE STUDIO

Initially one may be attracted to serigraphy for several practical reasons. Here is an art medium in which large size duplicate copies can be made in full color with simple equipment. No elaborate mechanical apparatus or complex techniques must be mastered. The serigrapher's studio may be confined to a basement, garage, attic, or even the kitchen table. He may purchase his equipment and materials at little cost, or he may choose to construct his own equipment.

In this chapter the physical space requirements and equipment needs of the serigrapher's studio are described. The necessary characteristics of the three essential tools, the screen, the squeegee, and the drying rack are explained. Methods for home construction of items to meet these needs are suggested. This can be easily accomplished by the amateur woodworker using only standard lumber

December Woods by Robert Burkert

and hardware items and common hand tools. Although care is required to produce satisfactory results, no particular difficulty should be encountered in making the screen or related equipment. My experience has been that assembling one's own equipment from the beginning is the most satisfactory solution to equipping the studio. However, equipment for serigraphy may also be purchased completely assembled and in various stages of assembly. Items available for commercial printing are priced relative to their mechanical complexity. Some screen supply houses stock screens suitable for fine art printmaking. Hobby kits for silk screen will soon be outgrown by the serious artist.

THE SCREEN

The two major components of the screen assembly are the *screen frame,* to which the screen fabric is attached, and the *baseboard,* the surface on which the copies are printed.

The *screen frame* and attached screen fabric carry the stencil. The fabric, usually silk, must be stretched drum tight on the frame to provide a firm support for the stencil and to resist rippling under the pressure of the squeegee action. Therefore, the screen frame members must be large enough in cross-section to prevent bending and warping under the stress of the tightly stretched fabric. The frame must also be rigid to resist racking, or distortion, during printing. Alignment blocks on the baseboard help eliminate frame movement during squeegee action.

The *baseboard* supports the printed copy during printing; the baseboard surface must be flat and smooth. The baseboard also carries the register tabs for accurate alignment of all stencils applied

FIG. 2–1
The screen assembly

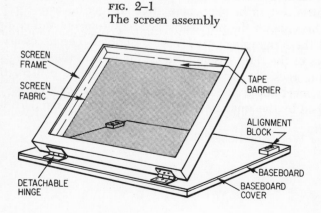

to each print; provisions must be made to maintain a constant relationship between the baseboard and the screen frame. While a common baseboard may be used for frames of different sizes, control over racking and stencil alignment is simplified when a baseboard serves only one screen.

A convenient method of removing the screen frame from the baseboard is necessary for cleaning, repair, and for some types of stencil preparation. Frame removal is usually required frequently during the production of a single print, and provisions must be made that will insure reattaching the frame in precisely its original relationship to the baseboard. Most frames are hinged to the baseboard with removable pin or other detachable hinges for easy removal and accurate replacement of the frame.

Silk, the traditional stencil carrier, possesses characteristics essential for a screen fabric. The strong, durable silk fibers can be woven to provide a fine, open mesh. Neither water nor strong solvents, such as acetone and lacquer thinner, damage the fibers or cause them to stretch or shrink. Synthetic fabrics have been developed for use on the screen; some of these, such as nylon, have proven suitable for serigraphy and may be substituted for silk. Screen fabrics are available in different mesh sizes. For fine art use, a mesh which imparts a minimum impression to the printed copy is desirable. The finer mesh weaves also allow rendition of more delicate detail in most stencil forms. For further discussion of screen fabrics, see "Notes" on materials for screen construction in this chapter.

Screen Construction

For many years I have used screens constructed as detailed here in my own studio and in my printmaking classes. This basic screen is simple to assemble, durable, and fulfills the essential requirements for an efficient printing tool.

As each serigrapher adapts his screen to meet his personal needs, he will evolve variations in screen design. I have included a few alternatives to the basic design and described several accessories as well. Other serigraphers and screen supply houses may suggest additional variations.

Screen Size

The first step in screen construction is to determine the size of the screen. The choice of size will depend on three factors: the maximum size print to be made, the size of paper stock, and the width of the silk or other screen fabric. The first factor is a matter of personal preference; the others may be affected by economy and availability.

Economical use of paper in whole or half sheets may be a consideration in determining print dimensions, and subsequently, the size of the screen. Paper suitable for printing is often difficult to obtain in large sizes. The largest standard size for index stock, a commonly used paper, is 25 by 30 inches. Most other smooth-surfaced art papers will not vary greatly from these dimensions. Card and cover stocks can be obtained in larger sheets but these materials are often less desirable in quality. See Chapter 3 for further information on printing papers.

Silk is available in widths of 40, 50, 60, and in some mesh sizes, 80 inches. The 40 inch width is the size carried by most art stores; the wider sizes may be ordered from a screen supply house. Other screen fabrics, obtainable in a variety of widths, are also available from screen supply houses. Table I gives several print and frame sizes for 40 and 50 inch silk in increments of 6 inch lengths. If intermediate lengths are obtainable,* the corresponding screen sizes can be computed. For easier stretching, the screen fabric should be slightly larger than the frame.

Screen Materials

When the size of the screen has been determined, screen materials can be collected. The following list includes those items needed for the basic screen. As an aid in selection of materials, some of their desirable properties are also noted.

---

* The policy of art stores in selling lengths of silk from the roll varies widely. Some stores will sell by the yard only, which often results in a considerable waste for the artist. I have persuaded several merchants to sell silk by the inch, or in increments of six inches, by pointing out that their waste at the end of a twenty-five yard roll will be negligible.

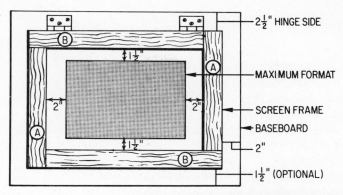

$2\frac{1}{2}$" HINGE SIDE

MAXIMUM FORMAT

SCREEN FRAME

BASEBOARD

2"

$1\frac{1}{2}$" (OPTIONAL)

TABLE 1: SIZES OF SCREEN COMPONENTS

Maximum format[a]	Outside frame size	Length of frame members[b] (4 ea. of A & B)	Fabric size[c]	Baseboard size[d]	Squeegee length[e]
12 x 15	19 x 23	(1x2) A-17½ B-21½	24 x 40 (2 pieces)	21½ x 27 23 x 27 (op.)	13
17 x 27	24 x 35	(1x2) A-22½ B-33½	36 x 50 (2 pieces)	26½ x 39 28 x 39 (op.)	18
22 x 31	29 x 39	(1x2) A-27½ B-37½	30 x 40 (1 piece)	31½ x 43 33 x 43 (op.)	23
26 x 39	35 x 49	(1x3) A-32½ B-46½	36 x 50 (1 piece)	37½ x 53 39 x 53 (op.)	27
30 x 39	39 x 49	(1x3) A-36½ B-46½	40 x 50 (1 piece)	41½ x 53 43 x 53 (op.)	31

[a] The largest size print that may be comfortably handled on the screen. This dimension provides ample space for manipulation of the color mixture outside the printing area.

[b] Each frame member is a lamination of two pieces. 1 x 2 finished lumber has actual dimensions of ¾ x 1⅝; 1 x 3 lumber is actually ¾ x 2⅝. The lengths of the frame members have been rounded off to the nearest one-half inch. Finished outside frame size will be slightly larger than indicated.

[c] Fabric sizes are for economical use of standard 40- and 50-inch roll widths. About one-half inch trim at the edges has been included for stretching.

[d] The minimum size baseboard allows space for hinges and alignment blocks; the optional size allows a margin in front of the screen frame.

[e] Squeegee length is one inch longer than the narrow dimension of the maximum size print for the screen.

Screen Frame

Frame members. See Table I for quantity and sizes.
1¼ inch nails for laminating frame members.
1¼ inch flat head wood screws for frame corners (8 req.).
Screen door braces or corner irons, with attaching screws (4 req.).
Silk or other screen fabric, 12XX or 14XX. See Table I for size.
¼ inch staples or ⅜ inch carpet tacks for attaching fabric.
Tape, gummed paper or clothed-backed, 2 to 3 inches wide.

Baseboard

Baseboard, ½ inch or thicker plywood. See Table I for size.
Baseboard cover, ⅛ inch smooth hardboard, such as Masonite, cut the same size as the baseboard.
½ inch brads for nailing baseboard cover to baseboard.
Removable pin hinges, 1 pair, about 3 inches.
½ inch flat head wood screws for attaching hinges to baseboard (6 req.).
1 inch flat head wood screws for attaching hinges to screen frame (6 req.).
Alignment blocks. Make from scrap pieces of 1 x 2 inch stock, or suitable substitute.
1¼ inch wood screws for attaching alignment blocks (4 req.).
$\frac{3}{16}$ inch flat washers for attaching alignment blocks (4 req.).
Finishes: shellac or other oil-resistant sealer.

Tools

Hammer.
Screwdriver.
Drill and drill bits.
Tack hammer or heavy-duty stapler.
Saw.
Square.
Sandpaper, medium and fine.

Notes

FRAME MEMBERS.   These should be cut from dry, straight, knot-free, medium soft lumber. For example, pine is excellent, since it is easily worked, resistant to splintering, and strong enough for all but the largest frames. Other warp-free woods may be used, such as fir, redwood, cedar, or spruce, if care is taken in assembly to reduce the hazard of splitting. If a stapler is to be used to attach the screen fabric, a medium soft wood is recommended, since some staplers will not drive a staple into hardwood. If carpet tacks are used, a harder wood may be suitable.

SCREEN FABRICS.   Silk, the fabric most frequently used on the screen as the stencil carrier, is available in a variety of qualities and mesh sizes. Vulnerable as it may be to sharp edges, good quality silk can take tremendous punishment, as indeed it must, during cleaning and from the wear and stress of printing. For this reason, it is worthwhile to obtain the best silk available for use on the screen. With reasonable care, such silk will endure for a remarkably long time. I expect a piece of silk to last through four to six editions, depending on the use it receives. In this time the screen will have been cleaned in several solvents and water from 120 to 150 times. Many stencil materials will have been introduced into its mesh and removed. It will have endured the abrasion of from two to three thousand squeegee strokes.

The life of silk will be shortened by accidental damage, careless handling, or improper cleaning. Discounting these, silk fails when the threads wear thin and break and runs develop. A small run will not give serious trouble in printing; the silk may hold up for several stencils or even an edition; however, it would be advisable to have an extra piece of fabric on hand. For, at any time, a run can become a hole which records as a prominent spot on the printed copy; then the fabric must be replaced.

Silk is coded by the coarseness of the mesh, from 6XX (double X) for very coarse to 20XX for very fine. The more open meshes are suitable for paper or film stencils, but to produce a smooth edge using a tusche or glue stencil, a fairly fine weave is necessary. A 12XX mesh is recommended as a good mean, suitable for a broad range of stencil types and excellent in strength.

Swiss organdy and silk organza are less expensive than silk but are coarser and weaker. They are satisfactory for cut paper and film stencils and for broadly handled glue stencils. Their capacity for delicacy and durability is inferior to silk.

Nylon offers the desirable properties of silk plus greater tensile strength. However, nylon tends to stretch and, while screen nylon is treated to minimize this characteristic, the nylon material must be stretched wet and pulled very tight, if the fabric is to retain its tension. Since the best quality silk is less expensive than nylon, nylon has marginal value as a substitute for silk.

Wire mesh has great durability and strength but is susceptible to denting by careless handling and the initial cost is high. Wire mesh is the most rigid of all stencil carriers and is capable of printing extremely fine detail.

TAPE.   A barrier of tape is often placed around the inside edges of the screen frame, lapping over onto the screen fabric to prevent the color mixture from seeping between the screen fabric and the bottom of the frame where it is extremely difficult to remove. If allowed to dry there, the mixture may abrade and eventually break down the fibres. A tape barrier also makes scooping up excess color mixture at the end of a run much easier. Gummed paper tape is suitable for use as a barrier if care is taken that the paper is not damaged in cleaning by the pick-up tool. A cloth-backed paper tape is more durable. I apply a narrow strip of cloth-backed tape, then cover this with a wider piece of paper tape—the double thickness provides additional strength at the most vulnerable place, the fold.

BASEBOARD.   The baseboard should be approximately three to four inches longer and wider than the screen frame to allow for hinge and alignment block attachment. The sizes listed in Table I allow generous space for these attachments; one could get by with slightly less. As with the screen frame, freedom from warpage in the baseboard is important. The frame, when placed flat on the baseboard, should make good contact all around. If not, uneven printing may result. One-half inch thickness is recommended as a minimum for the baseboard material. Plywood serves well; a little searching may turn up other good possibilities. I have an excellent board made from an old oak table top. Sometimes such pieces may be obtained at little cost from second-hand stores or charity outlets.

BASEBOARD COVER. Since variations of surface as slight as those caused by the grain of plywood may show up in the print, a hardboard cover is suggested to provide an extremely smooth surface for printing. A Masonite, Formica, or similar surface will also be more resistant to denting and scratching.

ALIGNMENT BLOCKS. Alignment blocks, fitting snugly against the sides of the frame near the front corners, prevent distortion of the frame during the squeegee stroke. These blocks are especially important on large screens to prevent misregistration.

Frame Assembly

1. Assemble each side member of the screen frame from two pieces of equal length. Stagger these a distance equal to the width of the member. Use a scrap or another piece of frame stock as illustrated to check adjustment.

2. Place frame corners together as shown. Use a square to check alignment. Pre-drill and countersink holes for 1¼ inch flat head wood screws and install the screws.

3. Turn the frame over so the corner screws are on the bottom. Install corner irons or reinforcing braces at each corner of the top surface of the frame with ½ inch flat head wood screws. Smooth ragged edges and remove splinters with sandpaper.

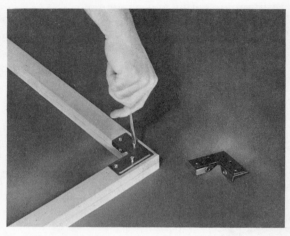

Attaching the Screen Fabric

1. Lay the screen fabric loosely over the frame and adjust for equal overlap at the edges. Tack the fabric to the frame at the center of one side with several carpet tacks or staples spaced about ½ inch apart.

2. Pull the fabric very tight and tack at the corresponding point on the opposite frame member. The tension should be so great that the fabric almost tears at the first tacks. Tack the center of the remaining sides in the same manner as the first two.

3. Work progressively toward the corners, stretching and tacking alternate sides a few inches at a time. When finished, the fabric should be stretched to an even tension everywhere and should be drum tight. Leave excess material until the finish has been applied.

Tape Barrier

1. Cut gummed paper or cloth reinforced tape to lengths equal
to the inside dimensions of the screen frame. Fold tape lengthwise,
gummed side out; dampen; and attach firmly, half on the screen
frame and half on the fabric. Smooth out all wrinkles carefully. If
cloth-backed tape is used, it should be covered with wider paper
tape. The smoother surface of the paper tape will make cleaning
easier, and a double thickness at the fold gives greater protection
against damage when the screen is cleaned.

2. If desired, the bottom of the screen frame may be covered
with pieces of paper tape to help prevent the entrance of color mixture between the silk and the frame. Allow all tape to dry thoroughly
before applying finish.

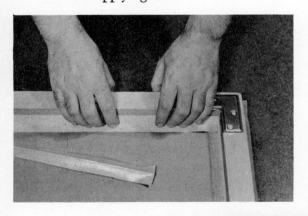

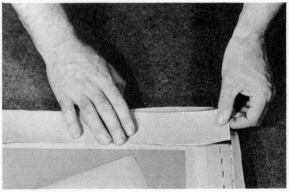

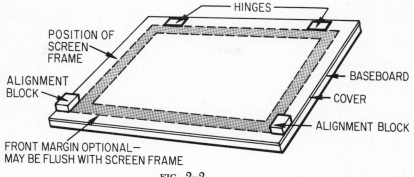

FIG. 2–2
Baseboard layout

Baseboard

1. Cut the baseboard cover the same size as the baseboard and nail the two together with ½ inch brads or nails near the perimeter.

2. Locate the hinges as shown in Fig. 2-2. Attach each hinge initially to the baseboard with one ½ inch screw. If necessary, install shims of thin metal or cardboard between the baseboard and the hinges to provide clearance for removal of the pins. Position the screen frame against the hinges and screw them to the edge of the frame. Install the remaining screws to attach the baseboard halves of the hinges.

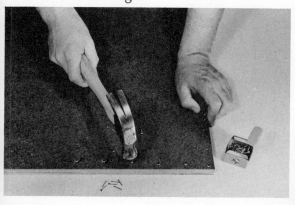

3. Fabricate two alignment blocks from pieces of scrap material. File or rout two elongated holes in each to allow for adjustment. Fit the alignment blocks snugly against the sides of the screen frame near the front corners (Fig. 2-2). Attach each block to the baseboard with two round head screws and flat washers. Position the screws near the center of the slots to allow adjustment in either direction. In use, if the screen expands (which it may do if soaked frequently in water during cleaning), or shrinks, or if the blocks become worn, loosen the screws, reposition the blocks snugly against the edge of the frame, and retighten.

Optional Hinge Attachments

If heavy stock, such as illustration board or composition panel, is to be screened, the hingebar attachment shown in Fig. 2-3 will allow adjustment for the thicker material. The hingebar, the baseboard support for the hinge, should be of the same thickness as the screen frame. The hingebar is attached to the baseboard with bolts and wing nuts. When thicker stock is to be screened, a shim of the same stock is placed between the hingebar and the baseboard, raising the frame to lie flat over the thicker material.

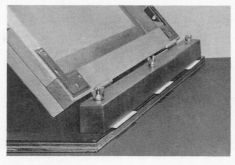

FIG. 2–3
Hingebar

FIG. 2–4
Hingebar brace

FIG. 2–5
Clamping hinge

At times the screen must be rested in a vertical position. When a hingebar attachment is used, a brace will be needed to support the frame when vertical. The brace shown in Fig. 2-4 was cut from aluminum angle and secured to the top of the hingebar by one of the bolts.

For rapid, convenient adjustment for thicker stock, a clamping hinge (Fig. 2-5) can be purchased or made. The hinge is screwed to the baseboard and the frame is held by the clamp. For screening thick stock, a shim is placed between the bottom of the frame and the clamp. Several frames may be used with the same set of clamping hinges.

Finishes

When screen assembly is complete, the screen frame, tape barrier, and baseboard should receive several coats of thin shellac, lacquer, or plastic finish. These preservatives are unaffected by most of the solvents used in cleaning and working the screen and are not damaged by prolonged soaking in water. Thin the finish to flow readily and brush on evenly. Sand lightly with fine sandpaper after each coat dries.

If the baseboard cover is a material which requires a finish, special care should be taken in coating this surface, as it will underlay the printing action and must be as flat and smooth as possible.

The screen frame should be finished past the inner edge of the tape barrier onto the screen fabric. The coating may be extended onto the fabric to the border of the largest print that can be made on the screen. If this is done, it will be unnecessary to mask or glue margins when making the largest size print, saving considerable time in stencil preparation. The finish should be applied to metal parts, such as hinges, nails, screws, and corner braces, to help prevent rusting.

When the finish is dry, wash the screen fabric with soap and water to remove sizing.

Screen Accessories

A number of accessories may be added to the basic screen. These simple mechanical devices increase convenience and efficiency and are worth the extra effort required in fabrication. Since the screen frame must be doused or soaked in water to remove glue stencils, metal used on the frame should be treated to prevent corrosion.

Sliding Bolt

At times it is necessary to prevent the screen fabric from contacting the baseboard—for example, during printing while copies are being hung to dry and during the drying period for a glue stencil. Both the color mixture and the glue are semi-fluid and may eventually creep if the screen frame is sharply inclined. A small sliding bolt, available in hardware stores, will serve to prop the screen frame a short distance above the baseboard and yet hold the frame flat enough to prevent the color mixture or glue from flowing (Fig. 2-6). This device eliminates the search for an unattached support which is usually just out of reach.

FIG. 2–6   FIG. 2–7
Sliding bolt   Prop

Prop

Another useful attachment is a prop which holds the screen frame high enough to allow manipulation of the printing paper into the register tabs (Fig. 2-7). Pivot a piece of wood or metal 6 or 8 inches long on the side of the frame about the same distance from the hinge line. The prop should swing freely on its pivot and fall automatically into place when the frame is raised, to hold the frame at an angle of about 45 degrees off the baseboard. To lower the frame, the prop is dislodged by hand. To place control within easier reach on large frames, the prop may be equipped with a wire link that extends to the front of the frame.

Handle

A piece of angle iron, a wooden cleat, or a handle, such as the common door pull or sash lift, can be attached to the front edge of the screen frame at the center to ease frame handling. While the frame can be lifted by grasping the front frame member, this may be tiring if the screen is large. Lifting with a handle also decreases the possibility of getting one's hands into the color mixture inside the screen.

Other devices will undoubtedly suggest themselves. Any accessory which eases the labor of printing can bring increased satisfaction to the printing activity. These devices usually will repay their construction time in more efficient printing operations.

THE SQUEEGEE

The squeegee is a device for spreading the color mixture over the screen fabric and forcing the mixture through the open areas of the stencil onto the paper. Of all the equipment used in silk screen printing, the squeegee is undoubtedly the item whose characteristics are most dictated by individual preference. The fit of the handle in the hand and the flexibility of the blade have very real consequences in the feeling of responsiveness to the screen during printing. With experience each printer will arrive at his own qualifications, but for the first selection, some characteristics can be recommended.

FIG. 2–8
The squeegee

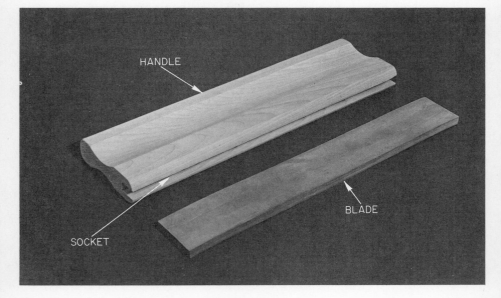

The properties of the blade should be the most important criteria in the selection of a squeegee. Flexibility is required so that minor irregularities in the printing surface will be absorbed by the blade, otherwise inconsistent copies will result. However, a blade that is too flexible will bend over when heavier pressure is needed and will feel sloppy and unresponsive in handling. To test the flexibility of an unmounted blade, hold the blade at its edges between the thumb and forefinger and try to bend the blade so it doubles over (Fig. 2–9). For blades under 24 inches the material should be stiff enough to resist doubling over even with a great amount of pressure. Upon release, the blade should spring back immediately to its original shape. If the blade is mounted in a handle, hold the handle in both hands and rest the blade on a flat, smooth surface. Incline and pull the squeegee toward you, applying force downward on the handle. You should feel the blade give slightly but it should not bend so much that the side of the blade contacts the surface; there should be a good deal of resistance and springiness.

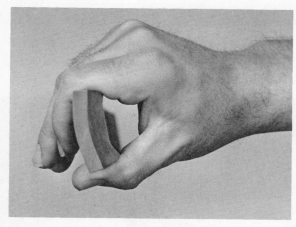

FIG. 2–9
Testing blade flexibility

Synthetic rubber or plastics are used more often than rubber for blade stock. One of the new blade materials available is a transparent amber plastic called Plasticol. This material is more expensive than other blade stock but is exceedingly tough and requires less frequent sharpening.

A blade of light-colored or grey material should be chosen since the wear during printing is less likely to affect the color mixture; the particles worn from a black blade can turn a light yellow mixture into a green within a few copies.

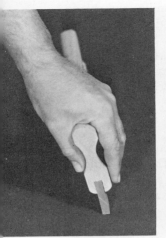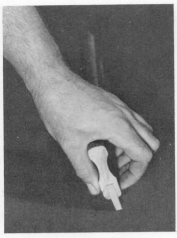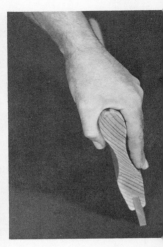

a. Good   b. Handle too shallow   c. Handle too deep
          FIG. 2–10   Squeegee handle depth

The shape of the squeegee handle, particularly the depth of it, should permit the fingers to straighten out comfortably without extending below the lip of the blade socket. Such a grip will allow maximum leverage and consequently will be less tiring (Fig. 2–10).

Squeegees under eighteen inches or so in length are sometimes equipped with a single vertical handle attached to the top center of the wooden strip that carries the blade (Fig. 2-11). These one-handed squeegees are pushed across the screen, rather than being pulled as are the two-handed squeegees.

The squeegee should be an inch longer than the narrow dimension of the maximum size print for the screen. To accomodate different sized formats conveniently, squeegees of different lengths may be kept on hand.

The finished squeegee can be purchased cut to size, in which case the charge is usually per lineal inch. Most art stores do not

FIG. 2–11
One-handed squeegee

carry a variety of handle sizes or blades of different degrees of flexibility. If their stock is not suitable, a screen supply house may fill special needs. On the other hand, the printer may wish to assemble his own squeegee. Handle and blade stock can be purchased separately in bulk at a saving in cost. Should replacement of either be necessary, the entire squeegee need not be scrapped. Handles may also be "custom made" to fit the hand.

Squeegee Assembly

1. Cut the handle and blade to the required length. Check the handle socket to see that it is smooth and straight. The blade should fit snugly but not tightly. Work the blade into the socket by hand. Seat the blade by thumping the blade edge against a clean, smooth surface. Sight along the blade to check trueness.

2. Nail a few brads about 6 inches apart through the handle socket into the blade from each side. Stagger the location of the nails on alternate sides. It may be necessary to drill small holes for the brads to prevent splitting the socket lip. Finish by applying shellac or lacquer to the handle only.

FIG. 2–12
Clamping socket

For easier removal of the blade, a handle can be purchased or constructed which clamps the blade in the socket (Fig. 2–12). A saw kerf is cut the full length of the handle, deep enough so the wood will bend without splitting. Screw-posts or nuts and bolts spaced about every 6 inches just above the blade socket squeeze and hold the socket sides tightly against the blade.

THE DRYING RACK

No less important than the screen itself as a major item of studio equipment, the drying rack provides safe and efficient storage for freshly printed copies. Inadequate facilities for drying can cause untold frustration and take a heavy toll of perfect copies from the edition.

When it is not otherwise occupied, many printers use their clothesline for hanging wet prints, but it is unlikely that this is the most convenient arrangement. A clothesline commands a good deal of floor space and may be awkward to fit into a studio plan. The clothesline may be made more efficient, however, by threading the line through holes drilled in the clothespins as illustrated (Fig. 2–13).

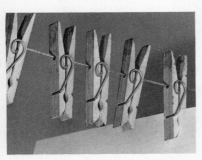

FIG. 2–13
Clothesline drying

A better studio device is the rigid rack, constructed of light lumber. The clothespins are attached to the rack by a nail inserted through the hole in the pin spring and driven into the edge of the rack member. If the nail is embedded just short of its head being tight against the pin spring, the pin will revolve freely and will fall naturally into a vertical position, regardless of the angle of the rack. Three types of rigid racks are described below.

The pole rack is braced at the bottom against the wall and anchored above on the wall with a cord running to a screw eye at the top of the pole (Fig. 2–14). Changing the angle between the rack and the wall will change the clearance between the copies slightly.

The frame rack employs the same principle, but instead of resting on the floor, the base is set on a window frame, ledge, or strip of wood tacked to the wall (Fig. 2–15). This rack is better for larger

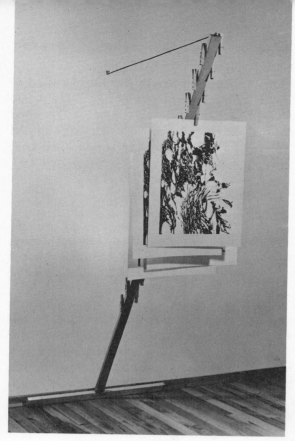

FIG. 2–14
Pole rack

FIG. 2–15
Frame rack

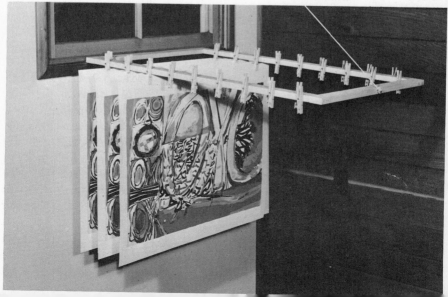

prints since they may be hung with two pins, one on each rack member. Such racks may be permanently built-in to fit the studio space or may be assembled in tiers for more efficient space utilization as in the mobile rack illustrated (Fig. 2–16).

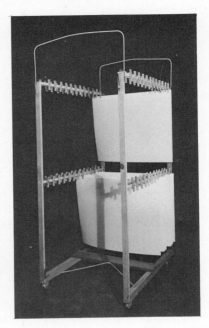

FIG. 2–16
Mobile rack

ADDITIONAL STUDIO EQUIPMENT AND LAYOUT

Few artists realize their desire for an ideal studio layout. Any medium requires a minimum area of operation; usually the more space available, the better for the efficiency of the artist. To overlap the clutter of one operation with another may be inconvenient for the artist as well as hazardous for the product. While the demands for screen work space may be modified to meet many conditions, certain minimum requirements must be realized. Knowing the critical elements will help in planning the work space arrangement. The newcomer to the medium may anticipate improvisations and compromises which may be necessary in his situation.

The screen needs to rest on a sturdy table, preferably accessible from three sides. The table need not be larger than the baseboard; the baseboard may serve as the table top. The height, while not critical, will depend on the size of the individual and the size of the screen. For printing, 36 inches is a convenient table height for an average or tall person working on a small or medium sized screen. So that one can reach across a larger screen, its table will need to be lower. Printing, cleaning, and stencil preparation are performed at the screen table.

To align stencils accurately in stencil preparation, one must have a line of vision at right angles to the printing surface. Such a view can be acquired by leaning over the screen from a standing position but in lengthy stencil preparation this stance may become tiring. A rack can be made to hold the screen at an angle, like a drawing board, so that work can be done on the screen from a sitting position. More simply, the screen can be rested on the lap and propped at an angle against the table.

When possible, a "clean" area should be set aside for paper and print handling, for matting, for stencil layout, and for storage of print editions, paper, and mat board. Activities such as color mixing and equipment construction and maintenance should take place in a separate area where tools, pigments, vehicles, and solvents may be stored. For convenience, the drying rack is located near the printing table. Provision should be made to store extra screens and drawing boards. One or two moveable tables are useful, particularly during printing, to hold the unprinted copies, squeegee, and other printing tools.

An ideal studio would have available a large wooden or metal basin in which the screen could be laid flat over a smooth bottom and soaked for removal of glue stencils. Since its use is relatively infrequent, this sink could be located outside the studio. I have substituted the garden hose with the nozzle adjusted to throw a high pressure stream on the screen, propped against a handy tree or the side of the house. All other screen cleaning, such as removing the color mixture after printing, is done at the printing table.

In addition to standard room illumination, an adjustable extension lamp near the stencil making activities is desirable. An intense light focused on the screen will also illuminate the copy underneath and will make registration of one stencil to another much easier.

3

PREPARING FOR STENCIL APPLICATION

Preliminary to developing the first stencil, a few simple procedures are necessary. The limits of the design area, or format, must be determined. Since the availability of paper may affect the choice of format size, edition and proofing paper may be selected and prepared for printing at this time. The format is laid out on the "working copy," the copy to which all stencils will be registered. Also, before the first stencil can be applied, register tabs must be attached to the baseboard. These will provide a means for maintaining a constant relationship between all of the printed copies and stencils.

Tide Pool by Warrington Colescott

FORMAT SIZE

The choice of format size is controlled at the maximum limits by the size of the screen. The area of the screen fabric left uncovered after taping and finishing the screen frame is the maximum area the frame is capable of printing. However, to attempt to utilize this full capacity would be extremely awkward and probably downright messy. Enough space should be left at the ends for manipulation of the color mixture at the beginning and end of the squeegee stroke. Enough space should also be left at the sides for the squeegee to cover the full width of the format area without riding on the tape barrier at the inside edge of the frame. The maximum sizes of the format areas listed in Table I are derived from the screen sizes, allowing generous space at ends and sides for manipulating the color mixture and squeegee. For screens of other sizes than those listed, use Fig. 3-1 to compute the maximum size of the format. Of course, smaller areas may be printed within these boundaries.

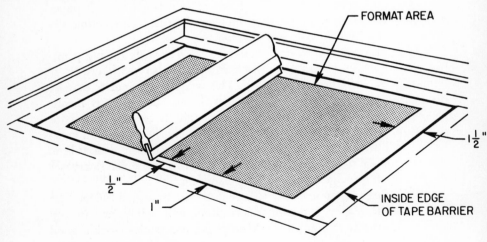

FIG. 3–1
Maximum format area

Economical use of paper in available sizes may affect the choice of format size. In computing format size to fit paper, margins must be allowed on the paper for registration, as described below.

PAPER

The paper used for printing should be of high quality and fairly heavy in weight. This "edition"* paper may also be used for trial runs of stencils and colors, or a lower quality, lighter weight paper can be substituted as a "proofing" paper. The proofing stock should receive the color mixture in essentially the same way as the edition paper.

Usually the edition paper should be smooth, but not glossy, or should have a very light tooth. Printing can be done on textured paper such as rough watercolor paper, if texture is deemed an important asset. However, difficulty may be encountered in securing coverage of consistent thickness. Some color mixtures change in appearance with variations of layer thickness; when a transparent color mixture is used, the paper texture may be accented by the heavier deposits of color in the depressions.

The paper should be dense enough to resist excessive absorption of oil from the color mixture. The blotter-like action of a soft paper will cause the oil to creep beyond the printed area, a distracting element, even though scarcely visible when dry.

The paper should be stiff enough to handle easily during printing. Papers heavy enough to resist curling are also less likely to be damaged by wrinkling or creasing. The weight of paper is usually designated by its weight per thousand sheets. "280M" thus means 280 pounds per thousand sheets. This weight is recommended for prints up to 25 by 30 inches. Larger prints may be printed on laminated stock such as illustration board which is regularly available in sheets up to 40 by 60 inches. The stiffness of this stock also decreases the danger of damage to the print by handling.

The most economical way to buy paper is through a dealer who sells in bulk. Paper company distributors will sell paper in full packages, usually of 100 sheets. Most paper companies stock a good

---

* The term *edition* designates all of the copies of the print that represent the final outcome of the artist's decisions for that particular graphic statement. All edition copies should be alike in representing the best state of the print. Other copies varying in appearance from the edition copies can be designated *proofs*, since variations usually result from trials of stencils or colors (see "Identification," Chapter 9).

quality index paper but usually in only one or two sizes. Area distributors can supply samples and prices for several weights of paper. A paper company may also carry an inexpensive index stock with appearance and printing characteristics similar to the higher grade index. This lighter weight stock makes excellent proofing paper.

Most high rag content artist's papers, such as drawing and watercolor papers, if heavy enough and not too rough, serve well as printing papers. Some can be purchased in bulk at a great saving in cost.

Unless the artist has a screen for each stencil, all of the copies printed must receive each color in turn; the decision of how many copies to make must occur before printing the first stencil. Losses may be expected during the process of printing. Mechanical mishaps, such as those described in "Printing Problems" in Chapter 7, handling damage, or miscalculations on stencils or colors will occur even with experienced printers. Thus, it is good practice to prepare a few additional pieces of edition stock above the proposed edition size. To complete the total, a half dozen or more pieces should be added for trial copies for proofing stencils and colors.

When the number of edition copies and proofs to be run has been determined, the selected paper can be cut to size for printing. Trim the paper to a size that will fit within the edges of the baseboard, without interfering with the alignment blocks or extending over the front. Allow a minimum margin of 1 to 1½ inches between the format area and the edge of the paper, more if possible. This margin is necessary to place the register tabs safely away from the squeegee while it is passing over the format area. At least two adjacent edges of the paper should be clean-cut to fit securely against the register tabs for accurate registration.

WORKING COPY AND WORKING PROOF

To provide a constant basis for planning and preparing succeeding stencils, a sheet of edition paper may be set aside to function as a "working copy." This copy, used as described in the following chapters, will serve as a guide for registration, as a cutting surface for the paper and film stencils, and as a guide for applying glue stencils. It will usually receive the first printing in each run.

To prepare the working copy, select one of the thicker edition papers and identify this on the margin as the working copy. Lay out the format area, observing the margin requirements described above. Draw the format border in dark line. Preferably, the layout drawing, if used, should be made on or transferred to the working copy surface, rather than be attached to it with tape or glue.

Once a few stencils have been printed, if they sufficiently delineate the layout, or if the printed image has deviated from the layout, it may be desirable to substitute a copy from the edition proofs for the working copy. The "working proof" will not have the layout drawing, which may detract from orienting each stencil to the printed image alone. The working copy may still be used as a reference and receive all printings, but the stencils are constructed to relate directly to the evolving image as printed.

REGISTER TABS

So that each print can be placed in exactly the same position under the screen frame to receive succeeding runs in registration, three register tabs are attached to the baseboard. The tabs should be anchored to stay in place until the edition is complete.

Of the types described below, the "Z" tab functions well with all except very thick papers or boards. The flap that extends over the paper makes the positioning of copies easier, especially if the paper tends to curl slightly. The flap also holds the edge of the paper down so that the copy will not be dislodged when the screen frame is lowered. Register blocks with flaps attached are useful for heavier boards which, even though thick, may tend to curl slightly. Disappearing guides or register blocks without flaps may be necessary for thick stock, especially if the printed area falls close to the edge of the stock.

"Z" Tabs

1. Cut three strips of medium heavy paper (such as scrap stock from edition paper) approximately ½ x 2 inches. Fold these into Z shapes with a short center section.

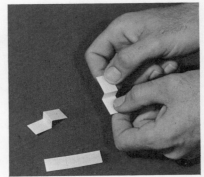

2. Adjust the working copy on the baseboard until the format area is centered under the open area of the screen fabric. Tape the working copy to the baseboard.

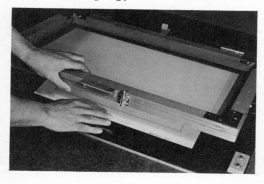

3. Slip one leg of the tab under the edge of the working copy. The lower fold of the tab should fit firmly and squarely against the edge of the copy. Position a tab near each end of the side of the working copy nearest the screen hinges. The third tab is placed at either end of the working copy near the corner opposite one of the other tabs. The tabs must not be placed in a position where they will deflect the squeegee as it rides over the format area.

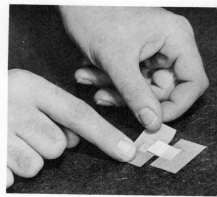

4. Fold each tab flat against the working copy and tape the top leg to the baseboard with masking tape.

5. Remove the working copy and tape the lower legs of the tabs to the baseboard.

Register Block

The register block is made from a block of material slightly thicker than the printing stock or from a piece of printing stock

FIG. 3–2
Register block

shimmed to provide additional thickness. If a flap is needed, it may be cut from a separate piece of thin metal or acetate and attached firmly to the block with glue. Small wire nails or glue hold the block or tab to the baseboard (Fig. 3-2).

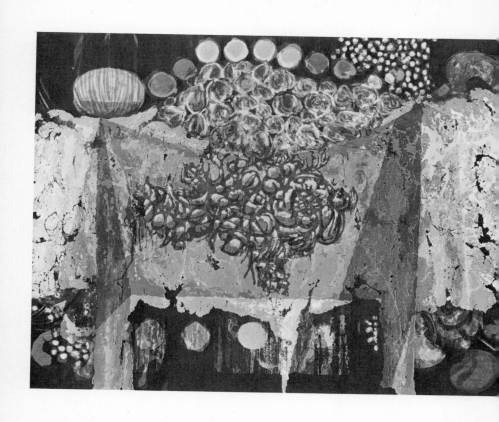

4

IMAGE FORMULATION

To paraphrase the definition in Chapter 1, silk screen is a means of developing and repeating an image by stencil. The artist is interested in the silk screen as a means of expressing an idea in an image. In this role, the medium can perform several services: it can serve as an adaptable and flexible means of transposing idea to image, it can contribute significantly to image form, and it can consistently duplicate that form.

To transpose one's idea to a visual image requires an allegiance of concept and means. While an idea often springs from an independent source, generally the characteristics of a familiar medium will influence the visual form the idea takes, even in the conceptual stage. The vision of an experienced artist will be influenced by his favored medium more than he may realize. Subconsciously he will select those characteristics of an idea stimulus that are in tune with

Interior Landscape by Joseph Fay

his most fruitful experience with his medium. He visualizes idea in an image form which may be capably served by his medium; in this sense, the medium is not a passive tool, but can engender image and often stimulates idea. A depth of personal involvement and a thorough understanding of the materials and methods of a medium are essential to its efficient utilization as an expressive tool. A balance of attention to technique and to expression is necessary of course— an imbalance results in superficial or clumsy pictorial statements. We can appreciate expert technique, even without significant idea content, or vice versa, but admire a high level of achievement in both technical facility and content.

The screened image is developed through a sequence of operations: stencil making, color mixing, and printing. As they occur in practice, each of these operations is usually separate in time but all are closely wedded by the dependence of each one on the others. None provides all the elements of the printed image form; for example, the design of the stencil is influenced by the characteristics of screened color and the printing method, and the color mixture is formulated to serve both the needs of printing and the stencil image. This chapter presents an overview of the interrelationships of these operations as well as a general description of the materials and methods of each. The techniques are described in detail in the following chapters. I suggest that this chapter be read first for an overall picture of the process and read again after some of the techniques have been tried. Conclusions stated here are drawn from my experience with the medium and undoubtedly reflect a personal preference for some methods over others. The medium may be used in diverse ways; while there is no single approach appropriate to all individual expressive needs, the following examination may provide useful background information for independent personal investigations.

For descriptions of each operation, names for some of the methods were invented to make cross referencing more clear; these names are for techniques or relationships that most serigraphers lump under a general title of "ways to get the job done." The terms are defined in the text.

STENCIL MAKING

Although the stencils do not reveal all elements of the image until printed, the serigrapher regards the stencil as his primary pictorial field. The stencils carry the image in an intermediate state between its concept and its final printed form, and become the major field of engagement between the artist and his idea. The transformation of idea to image may start directly with stencil making; even if preliminary drawings or layouts are used as guides for developing stencils, the stencil material and manipulation may still direct the transformation.

All stencil materials are applied to the screen in the unprinted areas of the image; the open mesh of the fabric will display the visual configuration of the idea, whose finished image form could easily be visualized even before the stencil is printed. When a print is composed of only one stencil, the problem of stencil design parallels that of a complete graphic statement in any medium. Printing the stencil would simply transfer the statement in pigment to a different surface.

While single stencil printing has attractions, one rarely finds it practiced, for few serigraphers can resist the compelling invitation of the multi-stencil print. Of the print media, the screen offers the least mechanical difficulty in printing color. However, the multi-stencil process adds this complexity to single stencil printing: the finished image is not revealed until all stencils have been applied. Each stencil contributes its particular elements to the final visual form; no one stencil can be considered inconsequential to the whole. Some stencils may be key stencils, with strong effect on the image, while other stencils act as more gentle modifiers; or all stencils may be of approximately equal importance. In any case, the image is evolved in sequential stages marked by intervals of stencil application.

This step-like progressive development has a very real influence on the image itself, and usually is the most critical factor to assimilate in becoming oriented to the medium. Whether the beginner will find this characteristic a continuing obstacle or will eventually have it working to his advantage will depend on his acceptance of the progressive development as inevitable to the nature of the medium. In the beginning, anticipating precisely the accumulative effects of each stencil on all others and forseeing the immediate effect of the individual stencil as it is being developed may seem imposing difficulties. The ability to sense the relationships of all the stencils will improve in time; early experiences in the medium may produce some frustration, especially if the print is too rigidly manipulated toward a preconceived form. With experience, the mechanics of combining stencils will grow less important, and idea and strategy will become more cohesive.

Approaches to Stencil Planning

With the idea budding and emerging, the serigrapher begins to plan his route toward a completed graphic statement in the silk screen medium. His approach may be spontaneous or controlled. He may start with the barest rudiments of a sketch, or he may develop a full color layout. He may let the results of each added stencil guide him in the formulation of the succeeding stencil or he may prepare careful color separations defining the configurations of all stencils before printing the first. He may follow one or a combination of several methods depending on his preference, the needs of his idea, the degree of growth the idea has had in form prior to starting the print, and the amount of experience he has had with the medium.

Color Separation Method

The color separation method requires a full scale rendering defining the final image intended. While most serigraphers do not attempt to adhere strictly to the appearance of this rendering, its qualities must parallel those that the screen is capable of printing. When the rendering is complete, a tracing for each color is made. These "color separations" may be drawn on acetate sheets with a sharp china-marking pencil or acetate-adhering ink. In this form, the tracings can be compared and adjusted to one another easily. The tracings are then used as guides for making stencils for each color. At other times, the first color separation may be made directly as a stencil, using the rendering as a guide. The color is printed, the next stencil is made and printed, and so on. In this more flexible method, color planning can be adjusted as the print evolves.

Series Method

The series method is also an approach that uses rather definite pre-planning, although not in the same sense as the color separation method. Instead of planning individual stencils, series or sets of stencils are anticipated. Each set is to perform a certain function. The stencil breakdown is not by color alone, but by kinds of visual activity. For example, the first sequence or set of stencils may have the primary function of establishing a movement pattern of a certain direction and kind. A second set of stencils, superimposed and integrated with the first set, may establish contra-movements. Other sets may then be used to develop specific hue character or activities, textural qualities, or value patterns.

Thus many variations are possible in planning by the series method. In form, the preliminary drawing may be a rudimentary sketch, perhaps even a diagram, which expresses not the details but the underlying organization of the image. The details are developed as printing progresses. Only a proposal for the general structure and a plan for its execution through sets of stencils would have been made before printing began.

The series approach is particularly useful when printing a large number of runs of transparent color, because the transparency allows the first stencils printed to remain visible through subsequent overlays, resulting in better integration between series. The approach is also especially adaptable to the series stencils described later in this chapter and in the following chapter.

Direct Method

A contrasting approach to the planned color separation and series methods, the direct method utilizes as idea sources the intrinsic characteristics of the screen and of the stencil tools. Planning is not absent from the development of the print, but is relatively less premeditated and is dependent upon immediate response to more random manipulation of the tools. Stencils may be developed purely for their own excitement quite apart from an image association. One or more early stencils may be developed in the same spontaneous spirit before controls are initiated to establish the final form.

It would not be sensible to propose that any of the above methods should be practiced to an extreme or exclusively. Any or all may be useful to fulfill the needs of an expressive idea. Even the beginner should not choose one as "the method I will use this time," but should responsively select the method that will vitalize or give control over his image at any stage of its development.

Mechanical Factors Influencing Stencil Design

The mechanical elements that delineate the possibilities and limitations of stencil printing are the transparency of color, the types of stencil combinations, the number of stencils used, the method of stencil preparation, and the method of printing. Color and printing are discussed in the next sections in this chapter; however, a definition of the degrees of color transparency is necessary here to clarify the descriptions of stencil combinations and methods that follow. The term *opaque* refers to completely opaque color which blocks out all underlying colors with one printing. *Semi-transparent* color dominates colors underneath, but is changed by the underlayers; several printings of the color would be necessary to block out the underlayer completely. *Transparent* color is extremely clear; all printings affect all other printings, and hue dominance is attained by tinting strength rather than by covering power (Fig. 4-1).

FIG. 4–1   Color transparency (in each example the circular figure was printed over the cross)

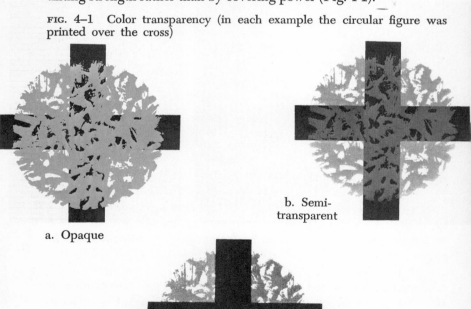

b. Semi-
transparent

a. Opaque

c. Transparent

Types of Stencil Combinations

Basically there are three ways stencils may be combined to delineate figure relationships; that is, three ways two or more stencils may define a shape against its background or other shapes. A stencil may have its printed areas related to the printed areas of other stencils in a side-by-side, or adjacent relationship; in an overlapping relationship; or in an overlaying relationship. The three combinations are usually intermixed in each stencil application; the choice of which to use depends upon the shape and color characteristics of the areas to be printed and the transparency of the color mixture. The types are not alternative methods of arriving at the same result.

Adjacent area stencils combine separately printed areas in a simple edge-to-edge relationship. For example, Fig. 4-2 illustrates

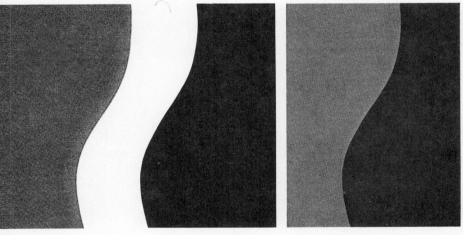

a. Stencil 1 print   b. Stencil 2 print   c. Stencils 1 and 2
                                                    printed in registration

FIG. 4–2   Adjacent area stencils

a shape developed with two stencils, the second stencil registered to the first along the edge. The printed areas of the two stencils fit together like pieces of a jigsaw puzzle.

If opaque color is used for printing, the first stencil is usually extended about ⅛ inch into the area of the second stencil. When the second stencil is printed, it overlaps and hides the edge of the first stencil. In this way registration is far less critical (Fig. 4-3).

When transparent color is used, if the second stencil overlaps the first as shown below, the edge of the first stencil will show

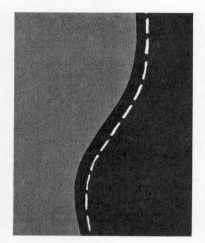   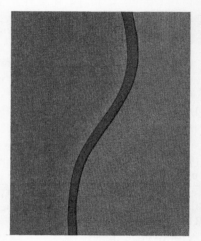

FIG. 4–3   FIG. 4–4
Stencil extension—   Stencil extension—
opaque color   transparent color

through the color printed with the second stencil, appearing as a ribbon between the two areas (Fig. 4-4). If this ribbon is to be avoided, the edges of the two printed areas must meet exactly. Such precise abutment is nearly impossible to achieve and maintain throughout an edition. For this reason, the adjacent area stencil combination is used less frequently in transparent color than in opaque color printing.

Overlap stencils, when used with transparent color, contribute to the delineation of additional areas and relieve some of the registry problems of adjacent area stencils. In Fig. 4-5, the central area is defined by overlapping the two parent stencils. The color of the over-lapped area will be a blending of the two stencil colors with a probable dominance of the second color. The value of the central area is usually darker than either of the other colors.

As the illustration shows, two overlapped stencils can produce a third color. Subsequently, three stencils can produce seven colors;

a. Stencil 1 print   b. Stencil 2 print   c. Stencils 1 and 2 printed in registration

FIG. 4–5   Overlap stencils

by adroit arranging, four can produce fifteen; and so on. It is impossible to take advantage of the liberal number of choices offered. I have been told by those who deal in mathematics that one could theoretically produce over a million variations by using a total of twenty overlapping stencils, over a billion with thirty!

Overlay stencils, similar to the overlap stencils in principle, differ in that one impression becomes the ground for the other. Overlay stencils are equally practical in either opaque or transparent color development.

The shape combination in Fig. 4-2, for example, might have been more simply developed through the overlay method illustrated in Fig. 4-6. With opaque color the printed results would be the same as those in the adjacent stencil method.

With transparent color, the first color printed in the example below would affect the second color overlay. Both the overlap and

FIG. 4–6   Overlay stencils

c. Stencils 1 and 2
printed in registration

a. Stencil 1 print   b. Stencil 2 print

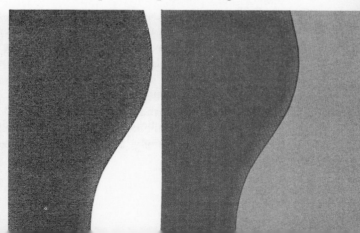

overlay stencil combinations require anticipation of the intermixing of the two layers of color to exploit the stencils fully.

Each of the stencil combinations—the adjacent area, the overlap, and the overlay—performs a somewhat different function in producing an image, and all are necessary techniques to make each stencil efficient. The paper, film, and glue stencils, described below, can utilize with equal ease any of the three stencil combinations. The only exception is the series stencil, which is usually an overlay technique.

Number of Stencils Used

While the number of stencils planned for a print influences the nature of the stencils to some extent, number is not usually a primary motivating factor in stencil design. To state the obvious truth, a serigraph requires as many stencils as are necessary to develop the idea completely. At the same time, each stencil combination should perform its job efficiently; proliferation adds little to print quality. When a third color or figure can be acquired through an overlap of two stencils, it would defy logic to use a third stencil for the same purpose. The number of stencils may be more important in the additive series (to be described shortly) when the open areas of the screen are blocked out progressively during a sequence of runs without removing the previous stencils. In this case, the rate of blocking out may definitely influence the number of stencils used in the series.

When using very transparent color, a certain number of over-layers seem necessary in order to achieve substance and depth in the color—to avoid a "thin-skinned" appearance. Clear transparent layers, when accumulated, grow deep and more luminous as more layers are applied. I have frequently used twenty to thirty stencils on a single print in seeking this particular quality, and have not felt the effort badly spent. The rewarding richness of such a combination is attainable only in the screen medium, which provides a controllable means for applying thin, even coats of transparent color.

Methods of Stencil Preparation

As an introduction, the basic stencil methods are described briefly below; additional information on their techniques may be found in the next chapter. Stencil configuration is developed primarily to meet the needs of the image form, but to duplicate this image the material used for the stencil must meet certain physical requirements. The stencil must be controlled in thickness to maintain a consistent paint film from copy to copy, be made with materials that are not damaged or dissolved by the color mixture, and be durable enough to resist the abrasion and flexing of printing.

The stencil materials described here are primarily those for oil color mixtures. Such colors are used far more frequently than water-soluble mixtures and are more adaptable to a wide range of image requirements. In addition, stencils for oil colors may employ a greater variety of materials that are generally more workable on the screen and easier to remove from the fabric.

PAPER AND FILM STENCILS. The paper and film stencils are cut stencils. In the paper stencil, holes are cut in thin paper in all the areas to be printed in one color; the remaining paper acts as the blockout for the color mixture. The film stencil is cut from a layer of lacquer laminated to a backing material. The areas that are to print are peeled away from the backing, leaving the backing paper intact to hold the stencil together until the lacquer film is adhered to the screen fabric, after which the backing is peeled away.

The image printed by cut paper or film will be exceedingly crisp, reflecting the incisive cutting action of the knife. The film stencil provides means to obtain more delicate areas than the paper stencil, since each piece of film is held securely in place until attached to the fabric. However, the film stencil is less easily varied from its characteristic clean, hard edge. With care, the cut form may be modified by burning with a hot iron, such as a small soldering iron or wood-burning tool, or the film may be partially dissolved with the adhering solution before or as it is being attached to the screen fabric. When cut, the paper stencil has much the same printed characteristics as the film stencil; however, paper is a much more flexible material when a variation from the cut form is desired. Paper can be torn, abraded, or burned. The stencil can be assembled from several parts, in the manner of a collage—the parts can easily be fixed in their proper place on the screen fabric. For additional variety in the printed image, papers of different weights and absorbencies can be used to vary the thickness of the color layer or to induce seepage of the color mixture through the stencil. The paper stencil is also less expensive and more rapidly produced, attached, and removed from the screen than film.

PHOTOGRAPHIC STENCIL. The photographic stencil is one in which a film of light-sensitive gelatine, attached to a backing paper or directly to the screen fabric, is exposed to light through a film positive or a drawing on acetate. The light reaches the gelatine film only through the clear portions of the film positive. The light and the developing solutions make the exposed gelatine insoluble in water. The unexposed, soluble gelatine is washed away to leave the open areas in the stencil.

Any dense opaque material applied to transparent film may serve as a positive for producing a photographic stencil. Reproductions of photographs, similar in appearance to reproductions by letterpress and lithograph processes, may be produced by the halftone method on the screen. A fine mesh is needed to reproduce fine detail and subtle value gradations; even so, the halftone dots will be relatively coarse, comparable to newspaper reproductions.

The photographic stencil is a reproduction technique that has had limited use in serigraphy. The artist's lack of interest has been due to several reasons; foremost among these is the detachment of the screen from image development. Whatever is being reproduced, the methods and materials used to delineate the image are little influenced by screen characteristics. The screen acts as a mechanical device for making copies rather than as an integral tool in developing image form. In addition, photographic stencils require special equipment and controls for satisfactory results; these are limitations which have not encouraged the interest of most artists in the specialized jobs the photographic process can do.

However, the photographic stencil should not be overlooked as a possible solution to image needs that cannot be readily satisfied by other screen techniques. If photographs, photograms, or particularly delicate or detailed drawings are needed in the image, the photographic stencil may well be an effective means.

GLUE STENCILS. Rather than being attached to the screen as are the paper and film stencils, the glue stencils are constructed directly in the screen fabric. Portions of the fabric mesh are filled with a blockout material, usually glue. A variety of printed characteristics is possible through use of various blockout materials and methods of application. Glue, the most frequently used blockout material, is easily applied and removed, has good brushing characteristics, and is fast drying. When applied correctly, glue stencils will print large editions without breaking down.

Other solutions that will serve to fill the mesh are lacquer and special screen blocking materials. All of these are similar to glue in that they do not dissolve in the solvents used in printing. In this text, I will use the term "glue" in a generic sense meaning all blockout materials that are applied directly to the screen fabric.

There are two major methods of constructing a glue stencil: by direct application and by applying glue over a resist material. Each method has many variations of technique. In each case the glue becomes the stencil, but the two methods differ in their influence on image form during stencil construction. I have found it convenient to call the direct application method a *negative stencil* method, because the glue is applied directly in all areas of the stencil that are

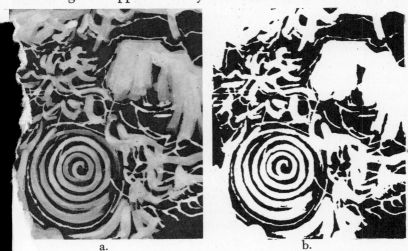

a.   b.

-7.   Negative stencil: a. The stencil—glue (white) is applied directly ureas that are *not* to print; b. The print

print (Fig. 4-7). It is then logical to call the resist technique ositive stencil method; in this method, wax is applied to the in all the areas that are to print (Fig. 4-8). The wax resists the

a.   b.

FIG. 4–8   Positive stencil: a. The stencil—wax (black) is applied to the screen in all areas that *are* to print; b. The print

glue that is spread over the screen fabric. When the wax is washed away with an appropriate solvent which does not dissolve the glue, the waxed areas of the screen will be open for printing.

In many ways the two stencil methods produce the same visual characteristics when printed. The sharpest distinction in their character results from their effect on the artist and, subsequently, on his handling of his image form during the period of stencil development. It is natural to think of the areas applied to the screen as the figure units, rather than as the ground areas of the image. This is probably carried over from working in other media—for example, it is not usual practice in drawing to delineate a figure unit by rendering only those areas around the unit. However, preparing the negative stencil is somewhat like this to the artist who is concentrating on developing his image in glue on the stencil and can apply the glue only in the nonprinting areas! Outwardly the negative stencil may seem a backward way of establishing an image. However, the artist should have little trouble with the negative stencil once he becomes adjusted to its printed form. He may find this type of stencil construction to his advantage in attaining an improved balance of figure-ground relationships.

The most common misunderstanding of the negative stencil is evidenced in attempts to use the method for effects more easily achieved with the paper or positive stencil. In practice the negative stencil requires a unique approach for efficient use; the artist must attend to what will remain of the previous image *after* the printing of the stencil in work. As he begins the stencil, all of the colors already printed will be visible to him on his working copy or proof directly below the tool he is using to apply the glue blockout. Those areas that he is covering with glue will remain as they are after this stencil is printed. All areas not covered with the glue will be changed.

In my own practice, I most often delineate the image in the negative stencil in much the same way as I do in the positive stencil. If leaf shapes are to be the image, leaf shapes are painted on the screen in glue more often than the areas around the shapes. However, the expected results are that the shapes will appear in the colors *already printed* rather than the color used to print that stencil.

The positive stencil method is more autographic and relates more directly with drawing and painting methods. The figure units of the image are established on the screen in wax; the image appears in wax as it will print. In application, liquid wax has much the same feeling and is applied with the same painting tools as casein or oil paint. The dry waxes, usually crayon or pencil, also have close association to similar materials used in drawing. Because the positive stencil relates more directly to familiar methods of developing an image than do other stencil techniques, I have frequently introduced and recommended the use of the positive stencil in initiating students to the screen process, even though it is technically more complex than either paper or negative stencil methods.

The glue areas applied in both negative and positive stencils can print a broad range of tonal variations through the use of different brushing techniques and glue mixtures. Dry brush, thinned glue mixtures, and application of textures make some degree of tonal gradation possible. Partially removing the glue, using glue thinned with water, or applying full strength glue to a dampened screen can produce areas of pinholes (minute openings in the stencil caused by glue shrinkage) through which the color mixture will seep and appear as lighter tones than in the completely open areas of the screen. Thus, areas may be printed which appear less flat and planilinear than with the cut stencils. Such glue applications may be most easily controlled in the negative stencil.

Textures can be introduced into the glue stencils by several means. The positive method utilizes a rubbing process. The textured material is placed under the screen fabric and dry wax is rubbed on the fabric over the textured material to deposit wax on the parts of the fabric that contact the material. The negative stencil method utilizes a transfer process. Glue is applied to the textured material with a brayer or brush, a transfer paper is pressed into the glue deposited on the high portions of the texture, and the paper is pressed directly onto the screen fabric. At other times, the textured material itself may be coated with glue and then pressed against the screen.

INDEPENDENT AND SERIES STENCILS. An independent stencil is developed as an individual unit, printed in a color, and then removed completely from the screen. A completely new stencil is developed for the next color. Cut stencils are usually independent stencils; glue stencils may conveniently be either independent stencils or series stencils. A series stencil is a member of a stencil set, a group of succeeding stencils modified progressively for several printings. A series may involve only two or three stencils or a half dozen or more. A series in which the second and each succeeding component stencil is developed by adding glue to the preceding stencil will be called an *additive* series. Glue may be partially removed from preceding stencils for a *subtractive* series; in this case the printed area will progressively enlarge with each stencil in the series. Each stencil printing overlays and adds to preceding stencil areas. A series may also combine both additive and subtractive techniques at separate stages or within one stencil.

The series method implies that some areas or edges will be common to consecutive stencils. The stencil at the beginning of a series may bear little resemblance to the stencil at the end, but common parts of intermediate stencils will provide transitional links that will tie together diverse changes to image form that may occur during the series. This is the major advantage of the series method—a better cohesiveness between stencil printings which generally gives better control over the image form. The series method also provides an efficient means for developing transitional passages in color and value. Registration and color fusion are relatively automatic between parts of a stencil series.

The following example of a series of two stencils traces the effect of this method on the image form: a portion of the image is painted on the fabric mesh in glue (negative stencil). This stencil is printed in red on white stock. After printing the edition, the color mixture is cleaned from the screen, leaving the stencil intact; more glue is applied to block out some open areas of the screen to make Stencil 2. Stencil 2, then, is a combination of Stencil 1 plus the added glue. Stencil 2 is printed in transparent blue, registered to the first printing. Since Stencil 1 had not been removed in making Stencil 2, the blue will not print on any areas blocked out by either Stencil 1 or 2. Furthermore, any edges of Stencil 1 that still remain as edges in Stencil 2 will exactly coincide in the two printings because the stencil and registration have not been changed. In this state, the print will have two colors plus the white of the printing stock. The white stock will appear in all areas blocked out by Stencil 1. Red, the color printed for Stencil 1, will appear in all areas that were added to Stencil 1 to make Stencil 2. The remaining areas, all that were left open on Stencil 2, will be a fusion of the two colors, in this case purple, because these areas received a layer of transparent blue over the red. It should be noted that in this example the blue will only be printed over the red, not over the white stock, since Stencil 1 was not removed during the series. The artist is relatively free of the necessity of establishing precise mechanical registration between the stencils since the physical presence of Stencil 1 in Stencil 2 insures automatic registration of the two.

The importance of the successive continuity of stencil development should be more obvious as more stencils are added to the series. A form can emerge in a progressive sequence through the series, in effect, displaying each stage in its evolution (see Fig. 5-10, Chapter 5). Furthermore, the visual activity of any stencil in the series can be varied from that of any other stencil, since elements of one are always retained in the next (Fig. 5-11, Chapter 5). For example, opposing movement patterns may be applied in succeeding stencils of an additive series; these patterns will combine smoothly through their retention of common elements. Series combinations may also exploit extremes of hue, value, shape, size, and texture; through the intrinsic transitional character of the series method the artist can maintain continuity between complex variations of form.

The series can be used to extend the single stencil into a more efficient form. A single stencil, individually developed and printed, establishes only one hue with a limited range of intensity and value. The basic stencil with slight modification can be printed again to vary the hue, value, and intensity. The modified stencil can be used to accent, sharpen or soften an edge, turn a plane or line spatially, or echo a configuration of the previous stencil. It is also some comfort to know that the considerable time and effort that may have gone into an individual stencil can be milked of greater potential than one printing can supply.

While the series stencil has these advantages over the independent stencil, there are disadvantages as well. The two methods are not alternative ways to produce the same result. The independent stencil offers the greatest utilization of the overlap stencil combination; thus greater multiplicity of color relationships within a given number of stencils printing transparent color is possible. Series stencils are strictly overlay combinations; the benefits of the overlap can occur between series, but not between individual stencils within a series. Also, the independent stencil is less limited in materials for its construction; these may contribute unique characteristics not possible with the glue stencils used in the series method.

COLOR MIXING

The color mixture and method of application determine the hue, value, intensity, and transparency characteristics of the printed image. The unique attributes of screen printed color can be fully realized only by the experience of printing color through the screen. Color is discussed here to point out some basic conditions that influence and control the mixing and printing of screened color. The first trials with the screen will further identify these conditions; experience will expose the more subtle interactions of each. The properties of the materials used in the color mixture, the methods of mixing, and the function and sequence of the color layers are among those elements that control the color form of the printed image.

Properties of the Color Materials

Color pigments are available in a variety of forms. Those most commonly used are screen process colors, tinting colors or toners, printing inks, artist's oils, and dry pigments. All pigment forms except the screen process colors are mixed with a base extender to obtain proper working characteristics for printing. Screen process colors are ready to use as purchased or may be extended.

Each color pigment will have a position on each of two different scales: *tinting strength* and *transparency*. Tinting strength refers to the coloring power of a pigment, often measured in screen printing by the degree of hue intensity the pigment retains after dilution with extender. Pigments differ greatly in native tinting strength; for example, phthalocyanine and oxide pigments are generally high in tinting strength, while cadmium and earth pigments are generally low or medium in tinting strength. The manufacturer's processing will also have some effect on the coloring ability of the pigment. Printing inks, which have a high concentration of finely ground pigment, will have more tinting strength for a given measure than the more coarsely ground pigments used in oil colors.

Transparency refers to the amount of light transmitted through a pigment layer. If a pigment is spread in an even layer on a white surface and bends (refracts) or reflects light to the extent that little light passes through the layer to the surface below, the pigment layer would be opaque. Some pigments are inherently transparent and offer less restriction to light passing through and reflecting back from the surface below. A color mixture containing opaque pigments will pass light relative to the amount of dilution with transparent extender; if the pigment is high in tinting strength, the color mixture can retain good tinting strength while achieving quite clear transparency. The combination of high tinting strength and transparency is ideal in a pigment to be used in mixtures for glazing. Unfortunately many pigments with these attributes fade or darken rapidly and are unsuitable. More information about the tinting strength, transparency, and permanence of pigments and extenders may be found in Chapter 6 and in the Appendix.

The reflective characteristics of printed color mixtures are qualities that a number of serigraphers have found useful in the development of image form. Some extenders and some screen process colors dry glossy while others dry mat. A mat surface can be made glossy with an overprinting of uncolored glossy extender; the reverse is also true—a glossy surface can be dulled with a clear mat extender. Mat and glossy finishes may be contrasted in the same print; the difference in their reflective characteristics can be used as a means of defining image. Metallic or fluorescent pigments or printing papers can also be used to obtain additional variety of color and luster in the printed image.

Methods of Mixing Color

Mixing of color on the slab prior to printing is a simple matter. Hue identity is determined by the component pigments, intensity by the purity and the amount of pigment used in the mixture, transparency by the relative proportion of extender added and by the transparency of the pigment, and value by the lightness or darkness of the pigment and also by the amount of extender used.

With an opaque mixture the printed color will be the same as that mixed on the slab. However, when any degree of transparency is used, the visual intermixture of layers of printed color becomes as important to consider as the colors being mixed on the slab. A factor often underestimated by beginners mixing a transparent color is its effect on colors already printed; or inversely, the effect of the colors already printed on the color being mixed. The determination of what characteristics of hue, value, and intensity a transparent mixture should have must be established through recognition of which areas the open areas of the stencil will cover. In addition, the color to be printed will not necessarily dominate the colors overprinted—a red printed over a blue may produce, depending upon the tinting strength and amount of red pigment in the mixture, a red-purple if the mixture is strong with red pigment, purple if the mixture is strong enough to balance with the blue undercolor, blue-purple if the mixture is moderate in red strength, or just a warmer blue if the mixture is weak in pigment.

The cumulative effect of color layers should not be overlooked in mixing transparent color. For example, a blue mixture that overprints blue will add to its intensity. The degree of intensity an area already possesses must be kept in mind as mixtures of like colors are being prepared. In the same manner, overprinting complementary colors will decrease the intensity of both the applied color and the color underneath.

Another factor to consider when gauging the strength of a transparent color mixture is the amount of competition a color will have when printed over other colors. A transparent mixture of great clarity which stands out sharply when printed alone on a blank white sheet may merge completely with the underlying colors already printed on the edition copies.

With the usual methods of printing, the color mixture for each stencil is deposited on the printing stock in a layer of consistent thickness. Each area will be printed in the same hue, intensity, value, and transparency. Apparent variations in the printed color can be obtained with both transparent and opaque mixtures by special stencil techniques. For example, stencil areas may contain pinholes which allow only small points of color to seep through. These points visually intermingle with the underlying colors, or with the white of the printing stock, to produce an apparent color change that resembles, in small scale, a broken color technique in painting. For similar apparent color variations, stencil areas may be made with hatching strokes or with textures. Opaque color mixtures must rely on these small juxtaposed color areas to produce an apparent variation of color within one stencil printing. Transparent color mixtures may utilize this method as well as their transparency.

Function and Position of the Color Layer

Each color layer may function in one or more of three ways: as an undercolor, as a major tinting color or "mover," and as a toner. In a general way these functions may also correspond to stages of image development, especially when transparent or semi-transparent color is used. *Undercolors* are preparatory colors applied with much the same intent as undercolors in painting. These are established early in the image development as a foundation to interact with later color layers. *Movers* are the main image delineating colors, usually employed at a stage when the artist is ready to move firmly toward the final pictorial form. *Toners* are modifiers, acting to nudge underlying colors without producing a major effect on hue character; consequently toners are often printed in the later stages of image development.

The distinctions in function are not precise and many color layers will have a dual purpose. With opaque color, a color may underlie later printings to facilitate registration; superimposed areas will cover some areas while appearing to abut adjacent areas of the undercolor. Opaque undercolors may be designed to interact in juxtaposition with small overlaying color areas to produce visual color mixtures. In the latter case the underlying color better fulfills the function usually implied by the term undercolor. Transparent color layers may fuse functions readily, becoming both undercolor and mover, or mover and toner within one application, depending upon how the tinting strength of the color mixture influences the image form.

An undercolor will often set the general hue and tone characteristics of the print and influence its luminosity. With any degree of transparency in the overlayers, the undercolor will modify the hue, intensity, and value of succeeding layers. Strong hue and value statements in undercolor are impossible to overcome with clear transparent overlayers, and semi-transparent mixtures will require several applications to completely eliminate the undercolor. If the artist is working with transparent colors, it will be to his advantage to understate contrasts in the undercolor if his approach requires flexibility in the configuration of his image at that stage of development.

Intermixing transparent and opaque color layers within one print sometimes creates awkward problems in maintaining visual cohesiveness between parts of the image form. The luminosity of opaque printed areas is distinctively different from areas developed in transparent color. Unless carefully related, an opaque area superimposed on a field developed in clear transparent layers will appear prominently foreign to the surroundings. For this reason artists usually use transparent or opaque mixtures consistently throughout a print, or, when both are used, the opaque color serves primarily as an undercolor for glazes with later stencils.

PRINTING

When the stencil is complete and the color mixture has been prepared, further image manipulation is possible in the final operation, printing. The choice of printing tools, the printing method used, and the surface on which the color layer is deposited will affect the printed form.

Printing Tools

The standard printing tool is the squeegee, equipped with a blade supple enough to absorb minor surface bumps and depressions during the printing stroke so as to distribute the paint in an even layer in all printing areas. The layer is thin, approximately the same thickness as the fabric thread, and will be constant in thickness in all printing areas if the blade can contact the open fabric mesh with nearly equal pressure at all points. A change in pressure will produce a change in the thickness of the paint deposit; even a slight change may affect the color, especially in transparent mixtures. Purposeful measures may be taken for controlled, repeatable variations in squeegee pressure, such as varying the stencil thickness or the base under the printing copy.

A dull squeegee blade that has edges rounded with wear deposits a heavier color layer and produces a more ragged but softer stencil impression than a sharp blade. If the color mixture is thinner than normal, a heavy layer deposited by a dull squeegee may be pulled into minute ridges and hollows by the fabric mesh when the screen is lifted; surface qualities produced consistently by this means may contribute to image form.

In the Orient a brush is widely used instead of the squeegee to spread the color mixture. The brush has been used successfully in reproducing watercolor paintings in France by a method called Pochoir. To my knowledge, the brush has gained little popularity in printing elsewhere, probably due to the greater skill and attention demanded for maintaining copy consistency. The tradition of using the squeegee has evolved in western countries; the brush has been unrecognized as a color applicator in a printmaking medium. However, the brush offers potential for image control during printing and, combined with the stencil, should be capable of producing adequate consistency between copies. The brush deserves more attention as a tool to augment the squeegee.

Printing Methods

The favored printing method for the majority of serigraphers is one that gives maximum copy consistency within the tolerances of a hand printing technique. A single, continuous, smooth stroke of the squeegee, applied with even pressure throughout, will attain that end. Variations of squeegee handling increase the chance of inconsistency between copies. A dependable method of darkening or intensifying a transparent color impression and of obtaining greater hiding power in opaque or semi-transparent mixtures is to return the mixture across the screen with a second squeegee stroke. This produces results similar to strengthening the color mixture for a single-stroke impression. Erratic squeegee action for depositing the color mixture irregularly gives less dependable control of the layer thickness from copy to copy. Some variation may be accomplished with consistency by applying different pressures to each end of the squeegee handle or by changing pressure within the length of the stroke.

An impasto or strong tactile variation of the paint layer may be achieved through a deliberate adjustment of one or several elements. Although a slight variation of paint thickness will occur naturally as a result of layer buildup, this variation may be increased by using a color mixture that deposits in a heavy film, a heavier mesh screen, thicker stencils, or several overprintings of the same stencil. The first utilizes what is called the "build" property of the mixture; some mixtures, such as many screen process colors or enamels which apply in a heavy film, have high build properties; other mixtures, such as tinting pigments extended with a large proportion of transparent base which apply in relatively thin layers, have low build properties. When stencil thickness is increased to achieve an impasto effect, the squeegee blade should not be deflected to a point where it cannot force the color mixture through the mesh onto the copy. Such deflection might prevent some areas from printing and load the mesh with an accumulation of mixture that will set and clog the mesh openings.

Another method for producing a heavy textural impasto utilizes a sifting technique. The screen fabric over the open printing areas is loaded with a heavy deposit of color mixture and the frame is jogged down sharply against the copy, sifting a deposit of the mixture through the mesh. Raising the screen draws the heavy deposit into pronounced ridges and valleys. The results will be generally similar from copy to copy, but variation in the textural configuration should be expected.

The Printing Surface

The material receiving the screened image influences the surface characteristics of the pigment film and will have a marked effect on the luminosity and color of transparent and semi-transparent mixtures. Paper is the most commonly used material for edition copies but other materials should not be excluded. Any flat material is suitable to print upon, providing the color mixture will adhere to it. However, the convenience of paper is indisputable, and the variety in texture and color available should satisfy most requirements. The texture and color will have only slight effect on opaque mixtures, particularly those with high build properties; the mixture will tend to level off the depressions and hide the paper color. With a transparent mixture, where layer thickness controls tonality to some extent, the puddles of mixture filling the depressions will visually accent the texture of the surface, progressively lessening in contrast as the areas become more deeply submerged under layers of paint. The color of the printing paper acts as an undercolor for transparent layers; colors other than white may decrease luminosity, which depends on the ability of the surface to reflect light.

The surface or base under the printed copy may also affect the printed image. A subsurface of varied thickness, constructed in the manner of a collage and placed under the copy during printing, causes much the same effect as variations in stencil thickness. Tests of this method indicate that a fair degree of consistency between copies can be expected if squeegee pressure is constant. When a subsurface is used, a fairly thin printing paper is necessary.

The following three chapters cover stencils, color, and printing techniques in greater detail. The descriptions of working methods are intended as guides for initial experiences with the medium. With practice, innovations of these techniques and others will be discovered that may better suit individual requirements. As beginning steps, I encourage experimentation with several of the stencil forms, especially the paper and glue stencils, and recommend development of the image directly in the stencil without preliminary planning. By printing a few proofs of all early stencils, the relationships of the operations, materials, and methods can be experienced. At first the process may seem reluctant to bend to the demands of image forms; this will happen with any unfamiliar medium. Let the medium control the image form for a while—mileage makes the driver more adept; with experience, the coordination of the mechanical elements will require less conscious attention.

5
STENCIL TECHNIQUES

The methods of making stencils described here are core techniques utilized by the majority of artists working in the medium. Some variations from the basic methods are also described—many more are possible. Of those materials used for fine art screen printing, two types are dominant: the cut stencil materials, usually paper or lacquer film, and the blockout solutions, usually glue. Variations of these materials, as well as variations in the ways they may be applied, will be discovered by the artist as his familiarity with the stencil making process increases.

PAPER STENCIL

Of the stencil methods, the cut paper stencil is perhaps the most simple. The stencil knife produces a smoother edge than the tools

South Dakota by Robert Freimark

used for glue stencils and allows more crisp delineation of fine delicate areas. The image printed from the cut paper stencil is strongly planilinear in character, due to its hard edge and uniform flat color.

The paper stencil can be made by methods other than cutting. To vary the incisive edge produced by the knife, areas may be torn from the paper or burned or abraded with appropriate tools. A soldering iron or wood-burning tool, such as the small heating iron supplied in hobby kits, is useful for burning lines and shapes. Abrading devices, which wear through the paper, will produce soft furry edges around open areas. For example, the paper may be placed over a texture and sanded lightly with fine sandpaper; the paper will wear through over the high points of the texture underneath. A puncturing tool such as a pounce wheel will rapidly produce a multitude of small perforations that may be used to create textures or broken lines or to direct the edge of a torn-out shape.

Stencils made from tissues, rice papers, or other absorbent papers allow a portion of the color mixture to seep through. Such leakage produces a softer and lighter impression than the completely open areas of the screen. If a constant squeegee pressure is maintained, the impression will be fairly consistent from copy to copy once the stencil paper has become charged with the color mixture.

Paper stencils require careful handling, as paper has a tendency to ripple during printing. For this reason, I find the paper stencil is best adapted to printing large units and use it primarily in the early stencils to establish broad undercolor areas. The paper stencil is also useful for masking out portions of glue stencils.

Materials

Stencil paper.
Stencil knife.
Sharpening stone.
Tape.
Glue.

Notes

STENCIL PAPER.   Any thin nonabsorbent or semiabsorbent paper may be used for the cut stencil. The paper should be transparent enough so that the drawing used as the guide for cutting can be seen through the stencil paper. Opaque paper is less suitable when registration is critical since an accurate outline of the areas to be printed must be transferred to the paper. Many papers sold as stencil paper are designed for the stencil brush and are usually too thick for screen stencils. A wax coating on stencil paper is also undesirable for use with oil-based color mixtures. A thin plastic-coated stencil paper would be satisfactory for screen use.

Tracing paper is a suitable substitute for regular stencil paper and is less expensive. Select a size of sheet or roll that will cover the entire dimension of the frame or, still better, extend to the outside edge of the frame. A tracing paper of medium quality is satisfactory. The least expensive papers are too brittle and may ripple excessively. The high quality papers have characteristics excellent for drafting, but not essential for stencils.

If a heavier deposit of color mixture is desired, a thicker stencil paper may be used, such as heavy stencil paper or drawing papers, or several layers of paper may be laminated. However, to print consistently without clogging, a very limited variation of thickness is possible. Moreover, the mixture will be deposited more heavily next to the edges than in the center of the stencil opening. More consistent layer thickness may be obtained with several overprintings of thin stencils.

STENCIL KNIFE. As with brushes and squeegees, the characteristics of the stencil knife are largely a matter of personal preference. The knife designed for cutting screen stencils, especially film stencils, has a cutting tip that swivels freely to follow slightly behind the handle. I use a small X-acto handle with the No. 16 blade. With this nonswiveling blade the knife handle must be revolved between the fingers when the direction of the cut is changed. With either style knife some practice is required to do a deft job of cutting. Regardless of which knife is used, the blade must be kept razor sharp.

SHARPENING STONE. A sharpening stone is an indispensable tool of the stencil cutter. A fine grained India or Arkansas stone is excellent. To sharpen a blade, lay the flat side of the beveled cutting edge against the stone and push the blade in a direction at right angles to its cutting edge, as if you were paring a thin layer from the sharpening stone. Keep the beveled flat of the blade fully against the stone at all times during the stroke. Make several strokes on one side, then turn the blade over and make several strokes on the other side. Use moderate pressure and finish off with several very light strokes on each side to remove the burr. Test by lightly scraping the blade across your thumb; the blade should catch the skin readily and feel crisp and sharp. When cutting the stencil, the knife should not plow a furrow, but should cut cleanly and easily without tearing the paper. The blade should be sharpened frequently during a session of cutting.

TAPE.   Masking tape is preferred for attaching the paper stencil to the screen. Transparent tape, which is thinner, is better for patching torn stencils.

GLUE.   To attach peninsulas and small floating areas use a glue that is water soluble when dry, such as LePage's Strength Liquid Glue, Original Glue, or Mucilage. The ubiquitous acrylic polymer glues in the handy dispenser bottles may prove difficult to remove from the screen without special solvents.

Making the Paper Stencil

1. Seat the working copy* in the register tabs and tape to the

---

* In the descriptions of stencil preparation, the terms "working copy" and "working proof" refer to the guides used for making the stencil (see "Working Copy and Working Proof," in Chapter 3). If color separations have been made, these are used as stencil guides.

baseboard. Cut stencil paper to approximately the same size as the frame and spread over the working copy. Align the ends of the paper with the ends of the frame and tape the paper to the baseboard. Indicate the areas that are to be printed by the stencil. The traced outline serves as a reminder only for the areas to be cut out of the stencil paper.

2. Using the working copy as a guide, cut out the areas to be printed. Cut directly over, but not through, the working copy. Lift out each section as the cut is completed.

3. Leave "floating areas," i.e., stencil areas that are detached from the rest of the stencil, on the working copy in their proper positions. Floating areas should be attached to the silk as described below. Peninsulas which need support should be handled in the same way.

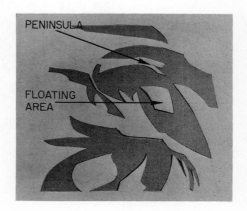

Attaching the Paper Stencil

The paper stencil should be attached to the screen just prior to printing. There is less possibility of misregistration if the frame with the stencil attached is not lifted from the baseboard until after the first printing. The color mixture will help adhere the stencil parts to the screen fabric.

Floating areas which are too small to be taped to the screen should be adhered with water-soluble glue. Larger floating areas may be taped to the screen, saving the nuisance of washing out glue after the stencil is printed. Tape should be kept a least ¼ inch away from the edges of the floating area; otherwise the added thickness may cause uneven printing through the adjacent open areas of the stencil. Adhesives exposed to the oil-based printing mixtures may eventually dissolve; however, most will hold up for all but very large editions.

Attaching Floating Areas—Glue Method

1. Carefully position the floating area in its proper location over the working copy.
2. Lower the screen frame all the way so the fabric contacts the stencil. Place a small drop of glue on the fabric directly over the floating area. Large areas may need attachment at several points. Press the drop of glue to force it through the fabric mesh. Leave the screen frame down until the glue has dried enough to hold the floating area to the fabric.

Attaching Floating Areas—Tape Method

1. Cut a slot near the center of the floating area. The slot should be about one half as wide as the tape. Turn the floating area over and cover the bottom side of the hole with tape.

2. Turn the area right side up and position over the working copy. The sticky side of the tape should be exposed through the slot. Lower the screen frame. Apply pressure to the fabric over the exposed sticky side of the tape.

Attaching the Main Stencil

1. If the stencil has been moved since cutting, reposition the stencil over the working copy on the baseboard and tape the stencil to the baseboard to prevent shifting. Place strips of masking tape at

the corners of the stencil, attaching one end of the tape to the underside of the stencil. The other ends should extend, sticky side up, beyond the edges of the frame when lowered.

2. Hold the stencil in place and carefully remove the tape that holds it to the baseboard. **Do not move the stencil.** Lower the screen frame. If the stencil has a tendency to curl, slip a thin ruler under the frame as it is lowered and flatten the curled pieces down.* After lowering the frame, attach the protruding ends of the tape to the frame sides. Attach the peninsula areas of the stencil with drops of glue applied to the fabric over the peninsulas, and press the drops through the fabric to adhere the paper. Do not lift the screen again until the first printing (on the working copy or proof) has been made. The color mixture will help adhere the stencil to the screen.

FILM STENCIL

The film stencil is a cut stencil which produces printed characteristics similar to the cut paper stencil. Work of greater detail, delicacy, and precision can be accomplished with film than with

---

* In extreme cases of curling, a second piece of tracing paper can be laid over the stencil to flatten it. This paper should be narrower than the stencil and stick out at the front or side of the frame when it is lowered. After the stencil has been attached to the frame the flattening paper may be slipped out.

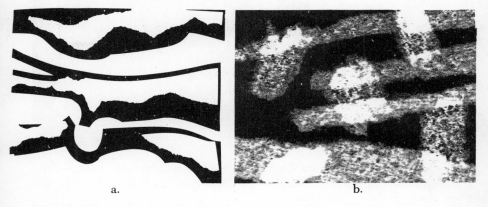

a.   b.

FIG. 5–1 Printed results of a paper stencil: a. Cut and torn paper;
b. Absorbent paper

paper because all stencil parts are firmly adhered to the screen over
their whole surface. Because of its greater expense and more involved application and removal, film is usually reserved for special
design needs or for when a large edition is to be printed.

Materials

Film.   Stencil paper or lacquer blockout.
Adhering fluid.   Masking tape.
Stencil knife.   Rags.

Notes

FILM.   Lacquer film consists of a thin lacquer sheet backed
with a sheet of transparent paper or plastic. The areas to print are
cut from the film and stripped away from the backing leaving the
backing intact to support the stencil parts until they have been
adhered to the screen fabric, after which the backing is removed.
Several brands of film are available, some with special adhering
fluids. The supplier should have instruction sheets for each brand;
these directions should be followed carefully. The process described
below is typical.
    Water-adhering film has similar cutting, adhering, and printing
characteristics to lacquer film with the exception that water is used

instead of a special adhering fluid. Water-adhering film is high in
cost but is safer to use than lacquer film which requires inflammable,
and sometimes toxic, adhering and destenciling fluids.

MASKING MATERIALS. Lacquer blockout, a prepared stencil
material, or tracing paper may be used to cover open areas of the
fabric beyond the edges of the film stencil.

Making the Film Stencil

1. Cut a piece of film slightly larger than the format area and
position it over the working copy. Tape the film to the working copy.

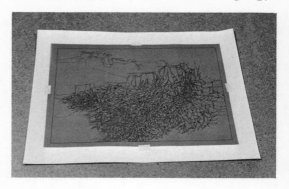

2. Cut around the areas to be printed. Cut only through the
lacquer film, not through the paper backing. Overcut corners slightly.
Peel off the areas of film that are to be the open areas of the stencil,
leaving the backing intact. Pick up any scraps or crumbs of the
lacquer sheet that lie within open areas.

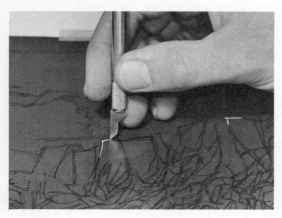

3. Make sure the screen fabric is thoroughly clean and dry. If it has been cleaned recently with kerosene, remove the oily residue with lacquer thinner or acetone. Cut openings in the film backing paper in the larger cutout areas to allow air to escape during adhering operations.

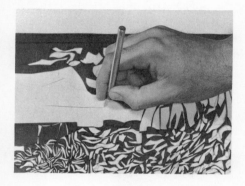

4. Register the working copy with the attached film stencil. Under each corner of the film affix tabs of tape, sticky side up. Remove the tape holding the stencil to the working copy. **Do not move the stencil.** Lower the screen frame and press the fabric against the exposed tape to attach the film temporarily to the silk. The frame and stencil may now be raised. Remove the working copy from the baseboard. Spread enough layers of newspapers on the baseboard beneath the stencil to assure firm contact between the fabric and stencil in all areas when the frame is lowered.

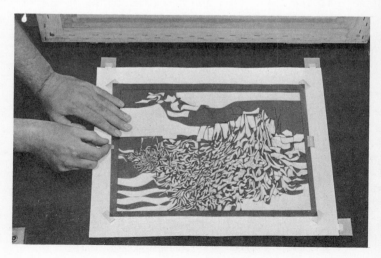

5. Use two rags, one dry, the other soaked in adhering fluid and wrung out. Starting at the center of the stencil, dampen a small area on the top side of the fabric with the wet rag. Immediately dry the area by rubbing briskly with the dry rag. When an area has been adhered, the color of the film as it appears through the fabric mesh will darken.

6. When an area has been adhered, move to an adjacent area and repeat the operation. Redampen the wet rag frequently with adhering fluid. Continue to adhere small areas at a time, working progressively outward toward the edges of the format area.

7. Allow the stencil a few minutes to dry thoroughly. Remove the tape tabs at the corners of the stencil. The backing may now be peeled off. Peel slowly, starting at the corners. Watch for tearing and improperly adhered film. If the film comes loose, repeat the adhering operation for that area before removing the backing. Mask the borders beyond the edge of the film with a paper stencil (see instructions for paper stencil attach-

ment in previous section) or apply lacquer blockout. The stencil is now ready to print.

GLUE STENCIL—NEGATIVE

The negative stencil is the most direct of all the stencil methods. The glue applied to the screen, upon drying, becomes the finished stencil. No intermediate steps, such as cutting or washing out, are involved. Different brushing techniques, glue mixtures, and applications of textures make possible a great variation of image form. Partial removal of the glue and the use of diluted glue produces areas of pinholes through which the color mixture will seep and result in a printed appearance that is lighter than in the completely open areas of the screen. Area edges printed from the brushed-on negative stencil are less crisp and appear softer than those produced by the cut stencils.

Textures can be introduced into the negative stencil by several means. The choice will depend upon the nature of the texture and the effect desired. Glue is rolled onto the textured material with a brayer or painted on with a brush. The texture may be pressed directly onto the screen or the texture may be applied by the transfer method. A texture effect is also created by the partial resist technique, in which the screen fabric is treated to resist the glue. These techniques are described below.

Materials

Glue or prepared blockout material.
Colorants: white or light colored tempera, casein, or watercolor.
Glue mixture.
Brushes, pens, and other application tools.
Textured materials.
Brayer.

Notes

GLUE. The glue used for any application to the printing area of the screen should be one that is easily dissolved in water after it has set. Many of the glues available today are waterproof when dry and therefore are not useable for making stencils. A glue such as Le-

Page's Original Glue or Strength Glue retains the necessary requirements for solubility. If there is any doubt that a glue will be suitable, apply some to a scrap of screen fabric, allow to dry thoroughly, and then try to wash the glue out. If it comes out easily, it will be suitable for stencils.

COLORANTS. Tempera or other water-based pigments can be added to the glue to make the mixture easier to see on the screen. A light color or white usually produces the best visibility. Make sure the colorant is water soluble when dry; some of the colors available, like some of the glues, are water soluble only in a liquid state. If in doubt, test the colorant before using it in the glue mixture.

GLUE MIXTURE. The glue and colorant are mixed for use as blockout material. The glue mixture used for direct application in the negative stencil requires rather critical adjustment in its proportions to provide total coverage in one application and good brushing properties. The final adjustment will necessarily be by trial. The initial thickness of both the glue and the colorant will vary by brand and freshness. Also, the desired thickness of the mixture is affected by the fineness of the fabric mesh. If mixed too thin, the glue will shrink in the openings of the mesh leaving tiny pinholes that will allow a small amount of color mixture to seep through. If mixed too thick, the glue piles up heavily and is more likely to crack and break down during printing, opening minute holes in the stencil. As a start, mix about two parts glue, one part colorant, and one part water. When mixed thoroughly, the solution should be about the consistency of light cream and should drop readily from the mixing stick. Test the mixture by applying an area to the screen fabric. The glue should brush on easily without piling up in thick globs. Allow the area to dry and inspect it against a strong light held behind the screen. If holes are present, thicken the mixture by adding more glue.

The glue mixture may be diluted purposely to encourage pinholes to develop, or a full strength mixture may be applied to a damp or wet screen for the same purpose. The pinholes allow tiny spots of color mixture to come through and the appearance of the printed area will be lighter than areas in which the mesh is fully open. The edges will also be softer and, when glue is applied to a wet screen, gradations in tone will occur much like graded washes in watercolor. A fair degree of control can be maintained after one becomes familiar with the appearance of the colored glue on the screen. When pinholes are used as an element in the stencil, a few proofs should be printed on scrap paper. In these preliminary printings the color mixture is forced into the tiny pinholes. After the openings have been filled, the printed results will be fairly consistent between consecutive copies, but may change slightly over the course of a large edition.

BRUSHES. Sable or other fine hair brushes are best for brush application of glue to the screen. The glue mixture has about the same brushing properties as casein or tempera paint; brushes appropriate for these materials will also serve stencil making. A worn sable brush is often a useful tool since the shorter worn outside hairs help stiffen the center portion and give it more resilience in the thick glue mixture. Round sable brushes (No. 2 and larger), flat lettering brushes, wash brushes, and bristle oil brushes are handy for glue application.

Several of the liquid stencil materials may be used in a draftsman's ruling pen to produce a thin, even line, somewhat crisper and more regular than a brush line. The ruling pen is limited in the range of line widths; in addition, the width cannot be changed easily within the length of a single line. Very fine lines tend to follow the pattern of the fabric mesh, resulting in a zig-zag appearance whenever the direction of mesh and line do not coincide. Glue used with the ruling pen will probably require thinning to flow satisfactorily from the nib. When used for drafting, the pen nib is kept fairly sharp; a sharp pen must be used with caution on the screen to avoid damage to the fabric. The point may be blunted very slightly on fine emery paper to lessen this danger. After use with glue, dry the ruling pen thoroughly to prevent rusting.

Occasionally other tools may be useful for glue application. Strips of cardboard, cut to the desired width, can be used for broad strokes or for covering large areas. Strip edges, coated with glue, can be stamped or slid on the screen to create crisp lines. Cardboard or balsa shapes attached to stick handles can be used as stamps to apply the glue mixture. While the brush and pen are the most reliable tools for controlled application, inventiveness, if it suits the expressive end, is encouraged.

TEXTURED MATERIALS. A collection of textures for transfer application may include appropriate natural materials such as grass, wood, or rocks, and manufactured materials such as fabrics, screening, and textured papers. These surfaces should be medium or strong in tactile prominence.

BRAYER. Soft rubber, vulcanized oil, or gelatin brayers are the most satisfactory for applying glue to textures, transfer papers, or directly to the fabric. Manufacturers do not advise using gelatin brayers in water, especially new brayers. However, I have used gelatin brayers in glue, then cleaned them in cold water, with no apparent harm. All soft brayers should be stored with the rollers safely away from contact with any object or surface.

Negative Stencil—Direct Application

If the working copy is to be used as a guide, it must be kept a safe distance below the fabric to prevent contact with glue which may seep through the mesh. Corrugated cardboard or mat board lifts, when used as described below, provide close, equal clearance between the format area on the working copy and the fabric, making stencil alignment easier. The screen frame need not be detached from the baseboard while the stencil is being made; the screen fabric will flex to absorb the thickness of the cardboard lifts if they are placed close to the format borders and not directly under the screen frame, where they would cause the hinges to bind.

1. Seat the working copy in the register tabs and tape to the baseboard. Place strips of cardboard around the border of the working copy.

2. Using the working copy as a guide, apply glue directly to the top surface of the fabric with a brush or other tool in all areas that are *not* to print.

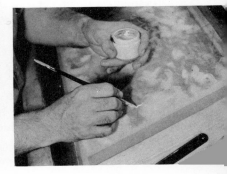

a. Full coverage

b. With a dilute solution

c. Dry brush and stipple

d. Glue applied to damp screen

FIG. 5–2   Printed results of a negative stencil, direct application

Negative Stencil—Transfer Application

In the method described above, glue was applied with the tool or texture directly to the screen fabric. In transfer application, an intermediate agent carries the glue to the screen. The glue impres-

85

sion from the texture is applied to a tracing paper or a wax paper. This, in turn, is pressed against the fabric. Since the texture material need not be regular or flat, textural effects not possible by direct application may be achieved in this way. Coarse, delicate, and extremely fine textures can be reproduced with considerable fidelity through careful application of the transfer method.

The transfer medium, if it is an oily paper, may contribute texture to the impression by resisting the glue and causing it to creep and bubble. Wax paper coated with glue reacts in this way.

1. Apply glue to the texture with a brayer or brush.

2. Press transfer paper, such as tracing paper, into the wet glue.

3. Transfer the impression immediately to the screen fabric. If the adjacent areas are to remain clear, the application may be confined to a specific area by masking.

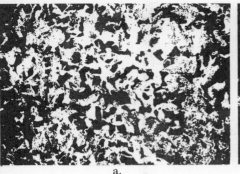 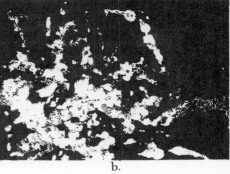
a.   b.

FIG. 5–3 Printed results of a negative stencil, transfer application: a. Tracing paper transfer from a texture; b. Glue painted on wax paper and transferred

Negative Stencil—Partial Resist

When applied to a waxy or oily surface, the water-based glue will draw together in bubbles. In the partial resist method, the screen fabric is treated prior to glue application with an oily liquid, such as kerosene or light machine oil, or with a soap solution. This resist causes the glue to creep, leaving openings in the fabric mesh. The degree and character of this reaction is controlled by the thickness of the glue and the oiliness of the resist.

To apply the partial resist, dampen the screen lightly with the resist (Fig. 5-4). Apply glue with a brush or other tool. If glue is also to be applied solidly in areas within those covered by the resist, remove the resist from the mesh with paint thinner and dry.

FIG. 5–4
Applying resist

FIG. 5–5
Printed results of a negative stencil, partial resist

Negative Stencil—Subtractive

The subtractive technique is a method of breaking down the total blocking of the fabric mesh by thinning or removing the glue after its application. The resulting textural and tonal variations are somewhat different from those printed through a glue mixture thinned before application. A combination of the two techniques is sometimes effective.

Several agents may be employed to pull the glue away from the fabric mesh. A piece of damp paper placed under the fabric will diffuse glue applied over it. Be sure to pull the paper off before the glue dries, however. Wax paper produces a different reaction and may remain in place until the glue has partially dried. Wet or dry paper may be pressed into the still wet glue from the top of the screen, then pulled away (Fig. 5-6).

FIG. 5–6
Pulling off wet glue,
subtractive method

If a specific area of dried glue is to be removed completely, apply clear water over the area with a brush, using as much water as possible without spreading beyond the area. Allow the glue to soak for a minute or two, then wipe the dissolved glue from the screen with a single stroke of a dry cloth. Do not scrub the area with the cloth; adjacent glue areas may be dissolved. Repeat the process if the first application does not clear the area. When only partial leakage is desired, shorten the soaking time to thin the glue. Edges of dry glue areas may be softened by gentle brushing with a water-filled bristle brush.

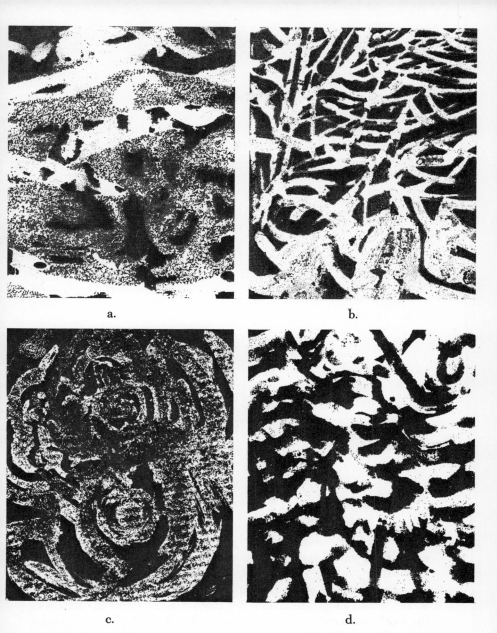

a.

b.

c.

d.

FIG. 5–7 Printed results of a negative stencil, subtractive method: a. Glue applied to the screen over damp paper; b. Glue applied to the screen over wax paper; c. Dry paper pressed into wet glue; d. Dry glue dampened and rubbed off

Whenever working from the top of the screen, take precautions against glue attaching the screen fabric to the working copy, either by raising the screen frame to clear the working copy or by covering the working copy with wax paper.

GLUE STENCIL—POSITIVE

In constructing this stencil, a wax is used to delineate the positive areas—areas that are to print. The wax is applied thickly enough to cover the fabric strands and to fill the openings between. A thin, even coat of glue is flowed over the whole area of the stencil. The wax resists the glue; the glue blocks the mesh only in the parts unprotected by the wax. The screen is then washed out with a solvent that dissolves only the wax, leaving the glue intact. The areas which were covered by the wax become the open areas of the stencil.

The visual characteristics of an area printed by a negative stencil and by a positive stencil are similar, since both employ glue as the blockout material. Differences can result from the tool used to delineate the area—a wax pencil or crayon compared to a brush—or because the artist is defining opposite portions of his stencil in the two methods.

The positive stencil is related to drawing and painting in its printed effect. Tools such as crayon and tusche handle on the screen much as they do on other surfaces. For this reason, the positive method is probably the simplest for obtaining lines and textures in the open areas of the stencil and for clarifying and accenting existing forms.

Materials

Glue mixture or prepared blockout material.
Liquid resists: tusche, wax resist, etc.
Stick waxes: wax crayon, lithograph pencil, etc.
Hectograph carbon.
Textured materials.
Brushes.
Cardboard.

Notes

GLUE MIXTURE. The glue mixture used in the positive stencil is thinner than that used for the negative stencil since two coats will be applied for the complete blockout. A glue mixture that is too thick is likely to bridge over more delicate areas of the wax and cause trouble in freeing the wax from the fabric. Start with about one part water to one part glue for the first coat. A few scattered pinholes are to be expected when the first coat is dry. If a heavy concentration of pinholes develops, add a small amount of glue to the mixture for the second coat. Colorant is not necessary.

LIQUID RESISTS. Tusche is the standard liquid wax used in serigraphy. There are brands marketed especially for the screen; lithographic tusche is also satisfactory. In their liquid state, those brands that are thinned with oil solvents are preferable. Use the tusche as heavy as practical for good brushing properties—about the consistency of poster paint.

Painting wax on the screen differs little from painting on paper. The fabric mesh offers slightly more resistance than most drawing papers. Also, painting with the heavier tusche solution may seem clumsy at first. However, once accustomed to the character of the material, the beginner is likely to find it enjoyable and sensitive. Wax should be brushed on evenly and thickly enough to fully cover the mesh. Gradations in tone visible on the screen due to variations in the thickness of the tusche will not reproduce in the print. All areas that are to be open in the stencil should appear as solid blacks in the tusche drawing.

Wax resist, used in ceramics, has painting properties similar to tusche, but is colorless and is difficult to see on the screen. Wax resist is much cheaper than tusche, however, and may be used for filling in broad areas, saving the tusche for areas where visibility is essential. Wax resist is water soluble until dry, when it may be removed with oil solvents.

Other nonwaxy liquid resists with varied application characteristics provide additional flexibility in developing image form. Rubber cement or the more fluid Maskoid can be applied in the same way as the liquid waxes. These are rubbed off the screen when the glue has dried. Neither should be left on the fabric for long periods of time or they will become difficult to remove. Heavy-bodied and syrupy, asphaltum varnish can be dripped and drizzled for fine thread-like lines or can be brushed on broader areas. Lacquer may also be used as a resist. Lacquer is similar in consistency to asphaltum varnish but more difficult to remove from the screen.

STICK WAXES. Any of the waxes in stick form may be used for drawing or for texture rubbings on the screen. Among these are lithograph crayon, china-marking pencil, and lumberman's crayon. Apply stick waxes heavily.

HECTOGRAPH CARBON. Controlled areas of wax from hectograph or spirit duplicating carbon can be transferred to the screen by drawing on the back side of the carbon lying wax side down on top of the screen fabric. Hectograph carbon is generally available only in 8½ x 11 inch sheets and must be spliced for larger areas. I use the following procedure: make an accurate tracing of the areas needed from the working copy. If attached to a hectograph master, tear the carbon from the master and trim away the unwaxed portion cleanly and squarely with the adjoining sides. Lay the carbon, wax side up, on the back of the tracing. Butting the edges, assemble enough pieces of carbon to cover the entire format. Attach the carbon to the tracing with drops of glue. Trim the assembly along the format borders, place it wax side down on top of the screen, and register it to the working copy by aligning at the borders. On the tracing, retrace the linear areas that are to print with a hard pencil, ball-point pen, or other suitable tool. Apply enough pressure to deposit the wax under the tool onto the screen fabric. Remove the tracing and carbons, apply glue, and wash out the wax in the usual way. The carbon stains the fabric badly, as well as the hands, but it is a useful tool in stencil construction.

TEXTURED MATERIALS. Textured material for the positive stencil needs to be relatively flat and, because it comes in direct contact with the screen fabric, should not be a material that can damage the fibers. Cloth and paper of assorted textures, wood, grass, leaves, and, if used cautiously, coarser materials such as sandpaper and wire screening are suitable.

BRUSHES. Brushes for the liquid waxes used for the positive stencil are the same as those used for glue in directly applied stencils. Clean brushes in appropriate solvents: paint thinner, turpentine, lacquer thinner, or water.

CARDBOARD.   Scrap pieces of cardboard or mat board about 3 x 5 inches (which may also be kept on hand for cleaning color mixture from the screen and squeegee) are used in the positive stencil process for squeegeeing glue onto the screen, an operation called "carding down." The cardboard squeegees should have at least one perfectly straight edge. A thin metal sheet may also be used for carding down, if the sheet has no sharp corners or rough edges. This tool may also be useful for flaking glue off the wax when it is being cleaned from the screen.

Making the Positive Stencil

1. If tusche or other liquid wax is to be used, place strips of cardboard around the format area to raise the screen fabric off the

working copy. If dry wax, crayon, lithograph pencil, or hectograph carbon is to be used, the fabric need not be raised, but it may be desirable to protect the working copy with wax paper. Using the working copy as a guide, apply the wax to the areas that are to print. Crayon must be applied heavily—a light coloring may not resist glue attachment. Apply tusche liberally for the same reason.

2. Allow the tusche to dry at least until tacky to the touch. Then remove the pins from the frame hinges and prop the frame level ½ inch or more above the baseboard.

3. Pour a portion of the glue mixture on the margin of the screen near, but not on, one corner of the format area.

4. Squeegee the glue over the stencil with the cardboard squeegee. Use light, even, overlapping, parallel strokes. When the stencil is covered, scoop up the excess glue and return it to the mixture jar.

5. Finish carding down with light, rapid strokes in both directions to level the glue to an even, thin layer. Examine the bottom of the screen fabric. No seepage through the mesh should be present. Allow the first coat of glue to dry. Apply a second coat in the same manner and allow to dry thoroughly.

6. Reattach the frame to the base-

board and clean the wax out of the fabric mesh with paint thinner
or kerosene, forcing the dissolved wax through the mesh onto newspapers below.

7. Any glue that remains on top of the wax should come off
when the wax is removed. Flakes not removed by the cleaning rag
may be scraped off with a thin, blunt blade or fingernail.

8. Stubborn spots of wax can be removed by scrubbing both sides of the
screen fabric in that area at once. As a
last resort, use lacquer thinner, acetone,
or brush cleaner, or soften the glue on
top of the area with clear water locally
applied. When cleared of wax, dry the
screen thoroughly. Look at the surface
against a light to check for pinholes. Fill
these with glue. Remove glue bridges,
which will appear slightly lighter in
color than the glue seated in the mesh.

While making a positive stencil is a
very simple operation, to insure a leak-
proof stencil and a clear opening of all
waxed areas requires a rather critical adjustment of several factors. If trouble oc-
curs, check each step in the operation.
First, the wax must be applied thickly
enough to isolate the fabric from the glue.

a. c.

b. d.

FIG. 5–8 Printed results of a positive stencil: a. Tusche applied with brush and ruling pen; b. Crayon; c. Hectograph carbon; d. Asphaltum varnish

Second, the screen must be raised to prevent any possible contact with a surface underneath that would cause the glue to seep through the mesh and under the waxed areas. Third, the glue must be thin enough to roll off the wax, or gather in small bubbles on top of the waxed areas, but thick enough to bridge the openings in the unwaxed fabric mesh. Fourth, the carding down should be deft and light in touch, and completed before the glue can become firm and tacky; too much pressure on the card will force the glue through the mesh; too little pressure may result in an uneven coating with ridges or heavy deposits of glue that bridge over wax areas. One or two trials with the positive stencil should be sufficient to demonstrate the relationship of these factors and provide some confidence that the

96

image developed in wax on the screen will retain its form on the printed copy.

Positive Stencil—Texture Rubbings

Most readers will remember the experience of duplicating the image of a penny by covering the embossed coin with paper and rubbing over it with a crayon. By this principle the textural configuration of many materials can be transferred into stencil form. "Found" materials with prominences in surface structure, such as fabrics, wood, sandpaper, leaves, and grass, and built-up or embossed surfaces can be simulated in the positive stencil impression.

The material is placed beneath the fabric and the fabric rubbed with dry wax. The wax is deposited on the fabric over the high prominences of the textured material, reproducing the image of its tactile configuration in the same manner as the crayon rubbed on paper placed over a coin. To become a stencil, the rubbed wax image on the screen is carried one step further; glue is spread over the screen, dried, and the wax washed out (in the manner of the positive stencil) to leave an image of the texture open for printing.

A fairly heavy deposit of wax is necessary to fill the mesh openings of the fabric. A light rubbing with the crayon will deposit wax on the top of the strands but will not prevent the glue from filling the openings between the strands; an overbuild of wax is necessary—the image in wax will appear much heavier than its printed impression. A knowledge of the amount of overbuild necessary will be acquired through experience. At first, expect only the heavier deposits of wax to become the open areas of the stencil.

1. Outline the areas to be textured on the screen fabric with a soft pencil.

2. Place textured material over the working copy in the applicable areas and lower the screen frame.

3. Rub dry wax, such as crayon or lithographic stick on the fabric over the textured material within the guide lines indicated. Finish the stencil by applying glue and washing out the wax as described in "Making the Positive Stencil."

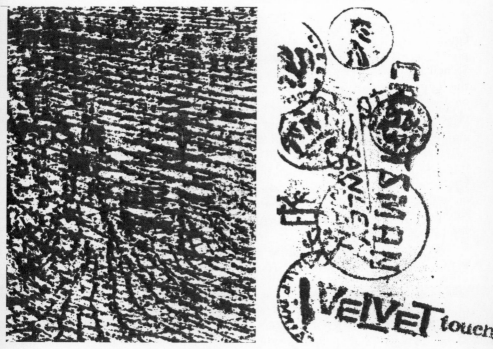

FIG. 5–9 Printed results of a positive stencil, texture rubbings

STENCIL SERIES

Outlined in Chapter 4 were several methods for developing stencils in series. The stencil series can provide greater control than the independent stencil in developing image form. A series may use one or several stencil techniques and may combine a few or many stencils; *series* implies only that two or more consecutive stencils retain some areas and edges in common. The common parts act as mechanical links between the variants of image configuration that may evolve in the separate stencils in the series. Series stencils utilize the same basic techniques for the glue stencils described earlier; factors especially relevant to the series combinations are discussed below.

Figure Pattern and Transparency

Successive stencils in an additive series can either modify a figure image established in preceding stencils or introduce completely new figure units. Fig. 5-10 illustrates a figure modification. Stencil 1 establishes a figure image pattern; Stencils 2 and 3 develop the figure started in Stencil 1. The development of the figure in glue on the screen parallels the evolution of the printed image quite closely.

As shown in Fig. 5-11, the figure developed in Stencil 2 may be a new figure pattern, introduced as an addition to the first figure pattern rather than as a modification of the existing pattern of Stencil 1. On the screen the stencil for the new pattern will be placed on top of, and appear to be in front of, the Stencil 1 pattern. When printed the image of the pattern in the latest stencil will appear to fall behind the images of earlier stencils. This reversed relationship between the appearance of the image on the screen and the image on the print may seem confusing in the development of the image form, but in reality the process can be a unique asset to the artist. He can build his image space from front to back; the first stencil prints the image of the frontal plane, the second stencil prints the next following plane, and so on until the last stencil in the series prints the farthest plane. Usually existing figures will be modified and new patterns added in the same stencil (Fig. 5-12), so that, through color inter-

a. Stencil 1

b. Stencil 2 (darker
areas added)

c. Stencil 3 (darkest
areas added)

d. Stencil 1 print

e. Stencil 2 print

f. Stencil 3 print

g. Stencils 1 and 2 printed
in registration

h. Stencils 1, 2, and 3
printed in registration

FIG. 5–10
Stencil series, figure
modification

100

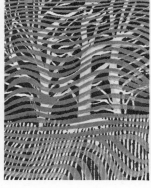
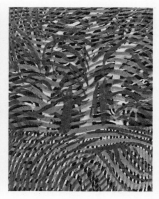

a. Stencil 1

b. Stencil 2 (darker areas added)

c. Stencil 3 (darkest areas added)

d. Stencil 1 print

e. Stencil 2 print

f. Stencil 3 print

FIG. 5–11
Stencil series, pattern addition

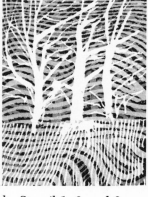

g. Stencils 1 and 2 printed in registration

h. Stencil 1, 2, and 3 printed in registration

changes occurring between components in the different layers, a
stiffly stratified appearance in the completed image is avoided.

The series offers means for deliberate and precise transitional
control over shapes and color. In each case the transition from one
state to another can be smoothed through progressive changes as the
series develops. Shapes can be transformed by steps in succeeding
stencils, and one color can gradate through intermediate hues to
another. These changes can be more naturally accomplished in the
series than in stencils prepared independently because the stencil

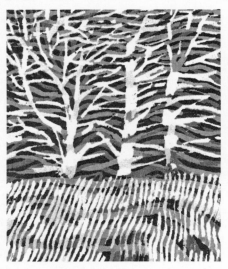

FIG. 5–12   Stencil series, combined figure modification and pattern addition

series is, as we have seen, a transitional modification from one stencil
to the next. Transitional changes in shape and line are controlled in
the stencil; color transitions by the color mixture and, in transparent
mixtures, by the interchange with colors already printed.

Since the series is an overlay type of stencil combination, transparent color will have similarities in appearance to opaque color.
Opaque color covers underlying colors—thus making more color range
possible within the series. However, the inherent fusing properties,
as well as the translucency, of transparent color combinations are

not available in opaque printing. A transparent color printed in the second stencil of a series will fuse with the first color; the combination will be analogous to both printed colors. In like manner, all succeeding transparent colors will fuse with those preceding. To utilize the desirable features of both opaque and transparent color in the development of certain image forms, I have found it useful at times to interlayer transparent and opaque color mixtures within a series (Frontispiece).

The printing sequence, the tinting strength of the color mixture, and the rate of blocking out the open areas of the screen are influential factors in controlling a transparent color series; the possible results attainable through varying all of these factors are endless. For example, a transition in color between red and blue will bring different results when the red is printed at the beginning of the series from when the blue is printed first, or when one pigment is mixed with a greater amount of extender than the other, or when the amount of glue applied covers more of the open areas of the screen in one stencil than in another.

At first a deliberate transitional development of one or two of the variable factors, leaving the others to chance, will introduce the potential of the series technique. While a careful analysis of all the factors will aid in predicting the outcome of the series, restriction to a rigid formula would seriously inhibit the expressive function of this stencil method. Rather than executing a tightly preplanned progression of moves, the artist should control the series development in response to his expressive end. As in chess, the strategy follows a concept, or master plan, but is modified through the response to the effect of each stencil on all preceding stencils.

Techniques for Stencil Series

The glue stencil is the most adaptable technique for use in stencil series. Glue is easily applied and removed and will remain imbedded in the fabric mesh undisturbed by the oil solvents used to clean the screen—an important factor enabling the stencil to retain perfect registry in succeeding printings of unmodified areas.

Direct application of glue (negative stencil) is the most efficient method for the additive series. Glue is applied to the open screen for the first stencil in the series, this stencil is printed, more areas are added in glue to the first stencil, this is printed, and so on. All preceding stencils remain present in the fabric; the additive series stencil can be viewed as a growing, rather complete graphic form in its own right. In the beginning the working copy or proof in registration directly below the stencil serves as a firm guide for applying the glue areas. As the series progresses, the stencils evolve relatively independently of the working copy underneath, for the glue obscures a major portion of this guide.

The positive stencil may be used exclusively in a series or it may be used in combination with the negative stencil. Wax is applied to the areas left open by the preceding stencil, the screen is coated with glue, and the wax is washed out. This process is repeated for each stencil in the series when wax is used to delineate the open areas. It is usually necessary to recoat the whole screen with glue for each stencil to assure adequate coverage. Because the accumulated glue layers may become too thick and crack, the number of positive stencils that may be used in a series will be limited.

The cut stencil cannot be excluded as a stencil technique for a series, but is not as handy to use. Each time the screen is cleaned after printing, the paper stencil must be removed, modified for the next stencil, and reregistered to the printed image—an act requiring delicate adjustment. The film stencil stays in the screen but is difficult to modify except by closing open areas with paper or glue. However, since lacquer film will not dissolve in the oil solvents or water, the film may remain in the screen through several successive printings of independent glue stencils. In this way the film image serves as a constant element between printings even though the other stencils in the series may have few common characteristics.

Materials and Methods

Although the stencil series utilizes stencil materials and methods described earlier in this chapter in essentially the same manner as independent stencils, several factors require special attention to accommodate the extended development of the series. These are related to mixture and application of the glue blockout and to cleaning between stencils.

Some areas of stencils in an additive series are likely to accumulate several layers of glue through many stencil modifications. Care should be taken that the glue mixture is as thin as feasible to insure complete coverage and at the same time prevent a heavy build-up when layers of glue overlap. If cracks do appear in a glue area, paint the area with glue on the underside of the screen. Broad areas to be solidly covered with glue may be applied initially with a thin glue mixture and the pinholes stopped out on the underside as well as the top of the screen.

When painting glue areas in a complex additive series, the artist may easily lose track of the sequence in which the areas he is modifying were printed. Once the glue dries on the screen it is difficult to tell which areas were just added to the stencil in work, and it is an arduous task to check each area with the proofs. The problem may be overcome by using a glue mixture with a different colorant for each stencil in the series. To avoid a large collection of glue pots, I usually start with a small jar of glue containing white colorant, mixed as described for the negative stencil earlier in this chapter. For the second stencil in the series, I add a little watercolor pigment, just enough to color the white mixture sufficiently to distinguish the newly painted areas from those of the first stencil. The hue may be varied progressively for each succeeding stencil by adding colorant to the previous glue mixture in the minimum amount necessary to produce an identifiable change.

A glue area that has been on the screen for several stencil printings should be checked frequently for leakage. Stencil glue properly mixed and applied to a clean screen should not leak for many hundreds of impressions, but often the conditions under which a stencil is made are not those ideal for long life. The stencil may have been purposely diluted to encourage pinholes; these areas may break down further after many printings. The glue may have been applied over a partial resist which prevented firm attachment to the screen fibers. Brushing action may have frothed the glue and formed tiny bubbles that finally wear through and allow color seepage. Such stencils may be adequate for one edition printing but not for several. Before each printing of a stencil in a series check all of the blocked areas on the screen and close newly-developed pinholes.

Special care should be given to cleaning and drying the screen after each printing. Even though it effectively blocks the color mixture from printing, the glue blockout is somewhat porous. In cleaning, the pores are charged with solvent containing diluted color mixture; if left to dry in the screen fibers, this mixture will be extremely difficult to remove after the glue is washed out at the end of the series. After each stencil is printed and the color mixture is cleaned out, the screen should be dried thoroughly to remove all solvent and mixture. Avoid leaving the glue stencils in the screen for long periods of time; whenever possible, complete the series and wash the glue from the screen within a few days.

OTHER STENCIL METHODS

The stencil techniques described above are those serigraphers have utilized most frequently. Potentially the photographic stencil may find greater use to serve special image needs. Also, due to the rapid technological development of synthetics, stencil methods for water-based pigments will undoubtedly receive more attention. The information about materials for the photographic stencil and stencils for water-based pigments below may provide a general familiarization for investigations in these two fields.

Photographic stencils are made with light-sensitive gelatine emulsions (see Chapter 4); these are supplied coated on backing materials or in liquid form to be spread on the screen. Art stores and screen supply houses carry several brands of photographic stencil materials. The necessary emulsion and its developing chemicals are supplied in kit form, or the components may be purchased separately. Instructions by the manufacturer will be included. Exposing and developing will require a moderate outlay of equipment to meet minimum needs, such as lights, developing trays, and exposure frames. Halftone reproduction requires camera and developing equipment that is usually beyond the means of the serigrapher. If he does not use the photographic stencil regularly, the serigrapher may choose to have the stencil prepared and attached to his screen at a commercial screen process shop where adequate equipment and experienced personnel are available.

If the color mixture to be used has a water base, many of the stencils in this chapter would not be appropriate, since these stencils materials would be damaged or dissolved by the mixture. However, the same construction techniques may be employed with different stencil materials in preparing stencils for water-based pigments. Of course, the tracing paper stencil cannot be used, but other plastic or wax-coated stencil papers are satisfactory. Lacquer film is waterproof and is one of the basic stencil materials for water-based colors. Lacquer should be substituted for glue as the stencil blockout material. Glue or tempera may act as the resist material in much the same way as tusche for oil-based mixtures, and may be washed out of the screen with water after carding down with a lacquer coating.

Most water-based pigments available produce flat, opaque colors, much like poster paints. There is relatively less opportunity to modify these characteristics than in oil pigments, which accounts for the greater popularity of the latter.

6

COLOR MIXING

The serigrapher will find a wide range of color characteristics in the materials available for the color mixture. Almost any hue, value, intensity, and transparency may be produced by mixing, and additional modifications result from printing in combination with layers of other colors. A clear transparent mixture requires finely ground, transparent pigment of high tinting strength. For semi-transparent color a greater range of pigments is available; almost any pigment that is ground in an oil vehicle can be used. If opaque color is chosen, screen process colors can be used as purchased and will cover thoroughly in one application.

My Window Facing West by Ivars Hirss
(Original Prints Gallery)

Mixture Materials

Pigments: printing inks, artist's oils, screen process colors, toners.
Transparent base.
Toner base, mixing varnish.
Mixing slab.
Mixing knives.
Tin cans.
Paint thinner, turpentine, or kerosene.

Notes

PIGMENTS. The ideal coloring agent for the transparent color mixture possesses a high concentration of very finely ground pigment. Printing inks have this characteristic, but may lack in the permanency required. Most art supply stores do not stock a high quality ink that has both high tinting strength and permanency. With some care in selection and reference to the manufacturer's rating of permanency, dependable printing inks may be acquired directly from an ink company.

Most artist's oils are permanent, and many are high enough in tinting strength to be utilized in transparent or semi-transparent mixtures. In addition, artist's oils provide a greater range in some colors, especially the earth colors, which may not be available in the inks, but must be simulated by mixing.

Screen process colors are ready to use from the can as opaque colors, or may be mixed with transparent base for semi-transparent colors. Screen process colors are available in a variety of vehicle combinations designed for special applications. The ones most frequently used by serigraphers are poster colors which dry to a mat surface and enamels which retain their gloss when dry. Even when opaque color layers are desired, the process colors may need thinning with transparent base, varnish, or paint thinner for good working properties in printing.

For clearer transparencies, the screen process toners or tinting colors may be used. These are more concentrated pigments designed to be used with extenders. Screen process colors and toners are available in a large variety of hues in several brands.

Additional information about pigments appears in the Appendix.

TRANSPARENT BASE.   The transparency and intensity of the color mixture is controlled by the proportion of pigment mixed with the transparent base. As it comes from the can, transparent base is a paste-like substance, composed usually of aluminum stearate and varnish, transparent amber or white in color. The major effect of the base on the pigment is in value and intensity control. Thus, a given amount of pigment will produce a progressively lighter and lower intensity color as base is added. Pigments vary in native tinting power and transparency as well. For example, lamp black, when mixed with many times its volume of base, will retain a stronger hue identity than ivory black mixed in the same proportions. Trial and experience will acquaint the printer with the relative amounts of base and pigment required for mixing the color needed.

Transparent base can be purchased in quart or gallon cans. Brands vary in color and consistency. Most bases dry mat.

TONER BASE AND MIXING VARNISH.   As supplied, most brands of transparent base are too thick for printing and too brittle when dry to build up more than a few layers without danger of cracking and flaking. Toner base has good binding properties, flexibility, and a low build, but is a syrupy substance, difficult to manage when used alone on the screen. A limited amount of toner base may be added to transparent base to improve its binding properties and flexibility while retaining the excellent working properties of transparent base. If further thinning is necessary, mixing varnish, which is thinner than toner base, may be added.*

MIXING SLAB.   A smooth surface, such as glass or linoleum, serves well as a slab for blending and thinning pigments before mixing them with base. A slab about a foot square is ample.

MIXING KNIVES.   A stiff bent-blade palette knife is an excellent tool for mixing pigments on the slab. For blending the ink and base mixture, an ordinary table knife serves well; the handle and blade of the table knife are long enough to reach to the bottom of the mixing can. A kitchen spatula is handy for picking up larger quantities of

---

* For example, Sherwin-Williams recommends the addition of 25 per cent Crystal Toner Base and 12 per cent Mixing Varnish to their Transparent Base. I have used up to 50 per cent Toner Base and Varnish. See "Preparing the Mixture" in this chapter.

base, especially when manipulating the color mixture during printing and for picking up excess mixture from the screen after printing.

TIN CANS. Tin cans are convenient and easily obtained receptacles for the color mixture. All sizes will find use, from small concentrated juice cans to large vegetable cans and, in the case of large editions, even two-pound coffee cans.

Quantity

Enough of the color mixture should be prepared to make all the printings in the run, including proofs. Remixing in the middle of a run usually results in unmatched copies. The amount of mixture needed will have to be learned by experience, since several variables are involved—size of the printed area, number of copies, and, to some degree, the thickness of the base.

As an example, let us say that a run is to be made on a 12 x 15 inch format. The edition is 20 copies plus 5 proofs. The open areas of the stencil total about half the area of the format. A 10-12 ounce concentrated soup can half full of color mixture, or a 15-16 ounce vegetable can a little over one third full, will be enough. About one third of this color mixture will be over-run. This is the supply of mixture left on the screen at the end of the squeegee stroke. Such surplus mixture is necessary to assure complete, no-skip coverage of the open areas of the stencil. The amount of over-run will not vary with the size of the edition, so if the number of copies in the above edition were doubled, less than twice as much mixture would be needed.

Preparing the Mixture

Screen process colors as packaged have a heavy, syrupy consistency. To obtain opaque color layers that fully cover underlying colors in one application, little thinning is possible. Workability may be improved by adding transparent base in small amounts; about 10 per cent will not seriously reduce the covering power of the mixture. To test the thickness, pick up a sample of the mixture with the mixing knife and tilt the blade to allow the mixture to fall back into the can. The mixture should drop off the knife easily but slowly.

For semi-transparent and transparent colors using toners, printing inks, and artist's oils, prepare the transparent base mixture first. A large quantity can be mixed at a time; I usually mix in one or two gallon batches. I use about three parts transparent base, two parts toner base, and one part varnish for a mixture which has good working properties on the screen. When adding toner base and varnish to transparent base, do not overthin the mixture. The consistency of transparent mixtures will test differently from opaque mixtures. The transparent mixture should drop off the knife readily in chunks. If a thick mass tends to stick to the blade, thin the mixture with varnish or paint thinner. If the mixture falls in a stream from the blade, add transparent base to thicken.

When preparing to make a run, fill a tin can with enough of the base mixture to print all copies and proofs. Mix the pigments to the desired hue on the mixing slab. Especially with the printing inks, a very small amount is needed for a brilliant hue. Add about a tablespoonful of base mixture and mix it thoroughly with the pigments on the slab before adding these to the remainder of the base. This step is very important; if the thick pigment were added directly to the base mixture in the can, it is quite likely that concentrated lumps and flecks of the pigment would not become thoroughly mixed and would cause streaks on the print.

The strength of the color mixture can be gauged by rubbing a thin swatch of mixture on a piece of printing paper. This should roughly indicate the intensity and transparency of the mix. To strengthen the color, add pigment; to weaken the color, add more base mixture. Before use, test and adjust the consistency of the color mixture as above.

Storage

At the end of the run, the surplus color mixture including the over-run can be stored for use in future color mixtures. Return all excess mixture from the screen and squeegee to the can and tap the can lightly against the table to settle the mixture to the bottom. Secure a wax paper cover to the top of the can with a rubber band. About six months is the maximum time the mixture can be stored and reused, depending on how much is in the can. If a scum develops, be sure to remove all of it before using the mixture (see "Printing Problems" in the following chapter).

7
PRINTING

Printing is the culmination of preparation that may have taken a good deal of time and effort. Now the result of the stencil design is finally revealed. Although the stencil determines the areas printed on the edition paper, and the color mixture controls the tone and color, printing influences, to a large degree, the quality of the surface and its fidelity to the intended image.

Only a few slight modifications to the image are usually executed during printing. These are accomplished mainly through the handling of the color mixture. With transparent color, variation of pressure on the squeegee will give a very slight variation in tone. Repeat running—that is, returning back across the screen with the squeegee stroke one or more times—will also affect the tone.

Shore Bird by Harry E. Krug

The primary intent is to duplicate on the edition paper exactly what is on the stencil. An effect achieved accidentally during printing, such as a skip, may make an unexpected improvement in the print, but this is a haphazard technique for design modification, difficult or impossible to repeat consistently throughout a run. If desirable, incorporate the effect of the skip in the stencil for identical reproduction in each copy. Printing accidents may suggest techniques which can be controlled and duplicated consistently.

Final Preparation for Printing

A few simple checks of the printing set-up should be made before printing begins. It is a nuisance to discover malfunctioning equipment during printing, and unfortunate if misregistered, streaked, or irregular copies have resulted; a quick inspection will expose trouble spots before they can cause harm. Until these procedures become habit, I recommend taping a reminder, similar to the check list below, to the exposed margin of the baseboard or to the screen frame.

SCREEN. Make sure the screen frame is securely attached to the baseboard at the hinges and both hinge pins are all the way in. When lowered, the frame should nest snugly between the alignment blocks, with no end play. Look through the screen fabric against a light for clogged areas in the mesh. Dried color mixture can be removed with a strong solvent such as brush cleaner or lacquer thinner; film can be removed with acetone or destenciling fluid; and glue can be removed with water.

SQUEEGEE. Sight lengthwise along the blade of the squeegee to check trueness. If any humps in the blade are detected, jar the blade with the palm of the hand at these points to seat the blade in the handle socket. Inspect the blade closely for nicks and dried particles of color mixture. The edges of the blade should be sharp.

STENCIL. If a paper stencil is used, the final step before printing is to attach the stencil to the screen frame. See "Attaching the Main Stencil" in Chapter 5. If a paper border mask is used with a film or glue stencil to stop out areas beyond the format, attach the mask in the same manner as the paper stencil.

Check List

Screen

1. Hinge pins secure.
2. Screen fits snugly between alignment blocks.
3. Open areas of fabric free from clogging.

Squeegee

1. Blade fully seated in handle socket.
2. Blade sharp, clean, and free of nicks.

Stencil

1. All areas to be printed removed from the paper stencil.
2. Stencil in correct alignment to working copy.
3. Check glue stencil against light for pinholes.
4. Border mask in place and leak-proof.
5. Paper stencil untaped from baseboard.

Squeegee Action

For printing, place the screen on a table at a height so the opposite end of the screen is within easy reach. Preferably the width of the table is the same or slightly less than the length of the baseboard.

    1. Pour a stream of color mixture across the far end of the

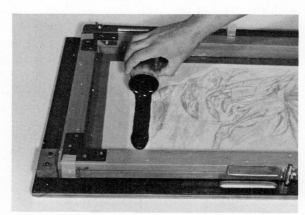

screen outside of the format area. Deposit enough mixture to make several strokes before replenishing is necessary. Always keep enough mixture on the screen to be assured of not running out and skipping spots during the squeegee stroke.

2. Stand at one of the short ends of the screen and slide the baseboard against your legs to prevent the screen from slipping as

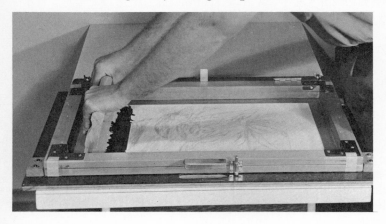

the squeegee is pulled across. Rest the blade of the squeegee between the mixture and the far edge of the screen fabric.

3. With both hands on the squeegee handle, apply pressure and draw the mixture forward. Tilt the squeegee slightly in the direction of the stroke. Apply enough pressure to distribute an even, thin layer of color mixture with no glossy deposits remaining. Amount of

downward pressure needed varies with the thickness of the stencil and the smoothness of the surface under the printed copy.

4. Pull the squeegee across the format area, stopping an inch or so beyond the near edge of the format. Examine the area covered by the stroke for skips, uneven deposits of mixture, or other irregularities (see "Printing Problems"). At the end of the stroke, drop the

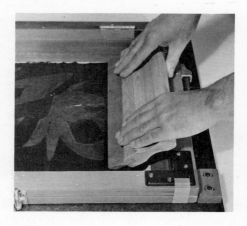

squeegee handle slightly as shown and slide the squeegee back a short distance (but not into the format area) to deposit excess mixture on the screen. This may also be accomplished by a few light taps of the blade against the screen fabric.

5. Lay the squeegee aside, lift the screen, and remove the working copy. If stencil or color changes are needed, make them now.

If color needs revision, be sure to include the mixture left on the screen and squeegee.

6. Insert the next proof in the register tabs. Tap the edges of the copy opposite the tabs to insure proper seating. None of the

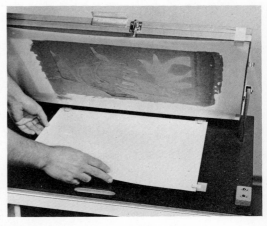

remaining prints need be attached to the baseboard—however, make sure they are not unseated from the tabs when the screen is lowered. Move to the opposite end of the screen and draw the mixture back across the screen. Continue printing, moving alternately from end to end for each copy printed.

Other Squeegee Techniques

The method of using the squeegee just described is a simple technique to control and may be the most natural for the beginner. However, it does require moving from one end of the screen to the other each time a copy is made. Printing from a position in front of the screen may save time and footwork. This position requires a little practice to retain an even pressure on both ends of the squeegee throughout the stroke.

When printing is to be done from the front of the screen, the screen baseboard should be securely fixed to the printing table. The printer stands at the center front of the printing area so that he may reach all parts of the screen. If the stroke is from his right to left, he extends his left hand to the far end of the squeegee resting beyond the right border of the print and begins his stroke (see Fig. 1-4). As he starts to pull the squeegee across the screen, he swings his body to the left in an even, continuous motion. Much of the motion will be in his torso, as he moves his arms independently very little. For the left to right stroke, the right hand is extended to the far end of the squeegee and the motion is reversed.

Some squeegees have a vertical handle at the top center of the blade support. These one-handed squeegees are designed to be pushed rather than pulled across the screen, and may be easier to manipulate from a position in front of the screen. The squeegee is held in the right hand for the stroke from right to left, and in the left hand for the stroke in the opposite direction (Fig. 7-1).

FIG. 7–1
Printing with a one-
handed squeegee

Printing on a very large screen may require two printers who pull the squeegee in unison down the length of the screen. One printer can manage a long, narrow screen when he has mastered the technique of walking the necessary number of steps without changing the pressure or stopping the movement of the squeegee within the span of the printed area.

Running the Edition

The proofs and copies in the edition are printed in turn. As each is printed, the copies are hung or racked so their wet surface will not contact other prints or objects. Print the proofs before running the edition; corrections are absorbed by the proofs so all copies in the edition will be perfect duplicates.

It is not necessary to print the edition in any definite sequence. However, if very precise registration is needed between stencils, such as exact alignment of delicate linear areas that are common to several stencils in a series, a printing sequence related to the direction of the squeegee stroke may be required. Even tightly stretched silk will ripple and shift very slightly under the pressure of the squeegee stroke. If an area receives two printings, one with the stroke direction opposite to the other, this shift may blur edges and cause extremely fine spaces in the stencil to fill in when printed. If several stencils have fine linear or textural parts that must align exactly for several layers of color, each copy for each stencil should be squeegeed in the same direction. To do this all copies and proofs may be numbered in sequence, and all odd numbers printed in one stroke direction and all even numbers in the opposite direction. Or each copy may be marked with an arrow indicating the direction of the squeegee stroke.

PRINTING PROBLEMS

Screen Clogs During Printing

SYMPTOM.   Lightening and irregularity in the printed area, usually increasing as printing continues.

REMEDY.   Place newspaper under the screen, scrub color mixture over screen fabric with squeegee, using as much pressure as possible. If mesh does not clear, rub lightly with a solvent-soaked rag and dry. Remove cause as outlined below.

Cause:	*To Correct:*
Not enough pressure on squeegee.	Use more pressure. Refer to "Squeegee Action."
Paper too absorbent.	Apply run of uncolored transparent base mixture, slightly thinner than regular mixture, to whole format area to reduce paper absorbency. Allow to dry before printing subsequent runs.

Color mixture too thick.	Use testing procedure outlined in "Preparing the Mixture." Mixture that is thin enough at beginning of run may thicken during printing as paper absorbs thinning solvents more readily than base material.
Color mixture dries in screen.	If color mixture has dried too hard to clear by method described above, cleaning with a strong solvent such as acetone, lacquer thinner, or brush cleaner may be necessary. Use method of cleaning dried pigment described in "Cleaning and Maintenance."
If trouble persists:	Check above remedies again, referring to appropriate text for more complete information. If trouble is accompanied by other problems, such as streaking, uneven printing, etc., refer to remedies for these.

Misregistration

SYMPTOM.   Double image or narrow gaps between areas from different runs. An inaccurately made stencil and a dimensional change in paper will show a consistent error between copies; other causes listed below will not.

REMEDY.   Remove cause as outlined below.

Cause:	*To Correct:*
Inaccurate stencil.	Always use working copy or proof as a guide for making stencils. Always work directly to runs previously made.
Play in screen frame.	Check for play at hinges. Adjust alignment blocks on screen. Snugness of fit may be affected by weather or by cleaning screen with water.
Print not seated in register tabs.	To insure full seating, make a practice of tapping printing paper lightly on edges opposite tabs after paper is inserted in tabs.
Register tabs loose.	Notice if tape holding tabs to baseboard has been loosened by solvent or if tabs have become worn and sloppy. Replace tabs or tape.

Too much pressure on squeegee.	Excessive pressure causes fabric to ripple; use less pressure on squeegee. If heavy pressure is necessary, note the direction of squeegee stroke on each copy and squeegee subsequent runs on each copy in same direction.
Loose screen fabric.	Restretch fabric.
Dimensional change in printing paper.	Accompanies a change in humidity; paper sealed in a package may need to be hung on drying racks for a day prior to printing to adjust to room humidity.

Color Mixture Runs Out Beyond Edge of Paper Stencil

SYMPTOM.   Feathers of color extending beyond intended printed area or format border.

REMEDY.   Carefully wipe mixture that overruns bottom of stencil clean with a cloth. Eliminate causes as outlined below.

Cause:	To Correct:
Too much pressure on squeegee.	Too much squeegee pressure will cause a paper stencil to ripple slightly. Depressions in the ripple become charged with color mixture which runs under the stencil and spreads as the blade passes over. Smooth out rippling that occurs, slitting persistent ripples and taping flat with transparent tape. Small ripples will not cause trouble if squeegee pressure is moderate.
Stencil torn.	Cover tear with thin tape, such as transparent tape.
Stencil damp.	Moisture will shrink tracing paper and make it useless as stencil material. Recut stencil on flat, dry paper.
Color mixture too thin.	Thicken mixture by adding base and pigment as necessary to maintain color intensity.
Excessive space between copy and stencil.	Pad underneath the printed area between the baseboard and copy to bring copy in closer contact with the stencil. Check frame and baseboard for warpage.

Uneven Printed Areas—Varies Between Copies

SYMPTOM.   Change of color or value of printed area that is not result of screen clogging. Varies from print to print.

REMEDY.   Remove cause as outlined below. If accompanied by screen clogging, clear mesh as described in "Screen Clogs During Printing."

Cause:	To Correct:
Imperfect squeegee blade.	Check squeegee blade for dried particles of color mixture and nicks, especially if the printed irregularity corresponds to direction of squeegee stroke.
Dried or poorly mixed color mixture.	Remove crust from end of pigment tube or from top of color mixture before using. Refer to Chapter 6 for proper mixing of pigment and base.
Color mixture too thick.	Color mixture that is too thick piles up on blade of squeegee, leaving insufficient mixture on screen to cover print. Thin mixture to consistency described in "Preparing the Mixture."
Not enough color mixture on screen.	Keep enough color mixture on screen to insure complete coverage without skips.
Uneven pressure on squeegee.	Screen should appear free of deposits of color mixture after squeegee stroke.
Uneven clearance between stencil and copy.	Usually the result of warpage in baseboard or frame, causing the fabric to lift from the copy sooner in one part than in another immediately after the squeegee stroke. Pad under copy with enough layers of paper to establish firm contact between the fabric and copy.

Uneven Printed Areas—Consistent in all Copies

SYMPTOM.   Change of value of printed area that is not due to screen clogging. Repeated with little or no variation in all copies.

REMEDY. Remove cause as outlined below. If accompanied by clogging, clear mesh as described in "Screen Clogs During Printing."

Cause:	To Correct:
Baseboard uneven.	Uneven surface of baseboard can cause part of the screen to become more heavily loaded with color mixture. Correct unevenness by padding with several sheets of paper taped to the baseboard.
Obstructions to squeegee.	Obstructions under blade of squeegee during stroke (often improperly placed register tabs) will lift the blade away from paper and vary amount of color mixture deposited.
Stencil too thick.	Paper: use thin tracing paper for stencil and format border mask. Glue: glue used in making stencil too thick, lumpy, or has seeped through mesh and dried on bottom of screen. Brush on clear water in the thick area, allow to soak a few seconds, and wipe off quickly with a dry cloth. Repeat as many times as necessary to remove excess.
Pinholes in glue stencil.	Clean screen with solvent, dry, and touch up pinholes with glue.
Dull squeegee.	Sharpen blade. Make certain that blade is not bending excessively during stroke.

Print Drying Time

Different brands and mixtures of color dry at different rates. The drying time of any one color mixture will be affected considerably by weather. No base will be constant in time needed for drying if the weather is fluctuating from cold to hot and damp to dry. Rub the printed area with a finger to test; if the surface is not thoroughly dry, it will feel soft and will drag against finger movement. Even the slowest drying color mixtures should set up enough to print over within half-an-hour to an hour. The surface may still be tender however, and extra care is required in handling. A paper stencil will tend to stick to a tacky print and may pull away from the screen fabric when the frame is lifted. Slender delicate areas of the paper stencil may actually tear. Generally it is best to allow extra drying time between runs of such stencils. The glue stencil offers no problem in this regard and may be used for overprinting as soon as the shine leaves the wet surface. Allow complete drying following the last run before stacking a finished edition for storage.

8
CLEANING AND MAINTENANCE

Cleaning up after a run may seem an anti-climax to the printing activity and a disagreeable part of the job. However, by spending a few minutes immediately after printing on a thorough cleaning of the screen and other equipment, an even more disagreeable job can be avoided—that of removing dried color mixture from the screen and tools.

Cleaning Materials

Solvents (see Table II).
Rags.

Newspaper.
Mild soap.
Bristle brush.

Black and White by Thomas Laursen

Solvent	Uses
Paint thinner.	Cleaning screen after printing, thinning base and color mixture, removing wax from screen.
Kerosene.	Cleaning screen after printing, removing wax from screen.
Turpentine.	Thinning base and color mixture.
Brush cleaner.	Removing dried pigment from screen, cleaning out extra-stubborn wax.
Acetone. Lacquer thinner.	Removing dried pigment from screen, cleaning out extra-stubborn wax, removing lacquer stencils and blockout.
Destenciling fluid.	Removing lacquer stencils.
Alcohol.	Removing and thinning shellac.
Water.	Removing glue.
Bleach. Household cleanser. Tri-sodium phosphate.	Removing stains from fabric, cleaning and degreasing fabric.

WARNING!

Some of the solvents listed above as well as some screen process colors and vehicles are toxic and should be used with great caution. Carefully observe the manufacturer's directions for use printed on the container. "Proper ventilation" means more than an open window. If toxic substances are used frequently, the studio should have adequate exhaust facilities. Great care should be practiced in the handling of inflammable materials as well. Cleaning rags should be hung to dry in an open ventilated area and waste rags burned or safely deposited to prevent spontaneous combustion.

Clean-up After Printing

In order to maintain the screen in good working condition, a thorough cleaning immediately after each stencil is printed is essential. Paper stencils must always be removed when the screen is cleaned. Film and glue stencils may remain on the screen if the color mixture is thoroughly cleaned out and the mesh dried of solvent, but it is advisable not to leave glue in the mesh for longer than a few weeks.

Immediately after printing, scoop the excess mixture from the screen with a knife or spatula and deposit in the mixing can. To store the mixture, cover the can with a wax paper lid fastened with a rubber band. Remove the paper stencil or border mask from the screen. The paper stencil is usually destroyed, but if it is to be saved for future use, hang the stencil to dry flat with the wet side free from any contact. A border mask may be reused many times.

Lay several thicknesses of newspaper between the screen frame and the baseboard. Douse the lowered screen with enough solvent (paint thinner preferred) to saturate the fabric and to completely liquify the traces of color mixture remaining on the screen. Rub the solvent through the fabric mesh with a rag. Enough solvent should

FIG. 8–1
Cleaning the screen after printing

be used to form a small puddle ahead of the rag as it is rubbed around the screen with some pressure (Fig. 8-1).

Lift the screen frame and wipe off excess solvent with a dry rag or newspaper. Use a rag to dry the screen fabric thoroughly, replacing the rag if it becomes charged with solvent. Continue rubbing until no trace of solvent can be seen on dry sections of the rag. Examine the fabric closely against a light. The mesh should be completely open. If areas remain clogged with color mixture, scrub these with two rags soaked in solvent, rubbing the clogged mesh from both sides simultaneously.

Clean the squeegee with solvent and dry the blade with a clean, dry cloth. Clean and dry the mixing slab and knives. Roll up the newspaper and rags and deposit them where they will not become a fire hazard, such as in a covered metal can, trash burner, or stove. Finally, dry the baseboard and the screen frame.

Glue Stencil Removal

The water-soluble glue stencil can be removed by immersing the screen frame in a tub or large basin of warm water, or by dousing the screen with a high pressure stream from a garden hose. Stubborn areas will usually loosen with soaking. A bristle brush can be used to encourage their disappearance. Soap will also help cut grease accumulations on the screen. Dry the screen fabric with a dry rag and check for clogging.

After a glue stencil has been on the screen for several days, traces of dried base that have seeped into pinholes or minute cracks in the glue may remain in the mesh when the stencil is washed out. These are deceptive since they are about the same color as glue and may be mistaken for glue; however all efforts to remove the traces with water will fail. Daub such areas with a little strong solvent, such as lacquer thinner, brush cleaner, or acetone, and rub them out with pressure applied simultaneously from both sides of the fabric.

Film Removal

To remove film, lay a piece of wrapping paper under the screen frame, making sure the paper contacts the screen fabric in all spots.

Soak a rag with distenciling fluid and rub briskly and thoroughly over the top surface. After a few seconds, lift the frame and pull off the wrapping paper. Clean the screen fabric thoroughly by rubbing simultaneously on both sides with fluid-soaked rags.

Stain Removal

The pigments and some of the stencil materials, such as tusche and hectograph carbon, may stain the fabric. This is not harmful so long as the openings in the mesh are clear. However, the stain may be distracting when one tries to develop a stencil accurately to the copy underneath. Subtle changes in value are especially hard to see through a bad stain. Strong solvents, such as acetone or brush cleaner, will reduce the stain, often enough to remove the problem. I have resorted to even more drastic measures on rare occasions, using a diluted solution of laundry bleach. A mixture, approximately 1 part bleach to 20 parts water, is doused on the screen laid flat over newspapers. The wet fabric is sprinkled with household cleanser and scrubbed lightly with a small bristle scrub brush. Five to ten minutes of such scrubbing usually eliminates all stains but undoubtedly reduces the usable life of the screen fabric as well.

Equipment Storage

If the screen cannot be left on the printing table, arrange suitable storage so the fabric will not be damaged. Vertical storage is best since objects which might cause abrasion cannot be piled on top of the fabric. When moving the screen, take precautions to protect the mesh from puncture or snagging.

Store the squeegee so the blade cannot contact other objects. A screw eye in the end of the handle provides a simple means for hanging. Treat the squeegee as a quality tool. A damaged blade can render it useless for printing.

Maintenance

Each printing session should be preceded by a quick check of equipment to assure trouble-free operation. The following maintenance procedures are recommended "rituals" for performance before each run.

SQUEEGEE.   Check the blade carefully for nicks, cuts, or irregularities. The blade must be kept sharp and true at all times (see Fig. 2-12). A sharp squeegee blade is essential for crisp, even printing. The blade should be sharpened after every few sessions of printing; more often if many copies are being made. A simple sharpener may be made by attaching a long strip of fine sandpaper, such as a belt sander strip, to a board or table (Fig. 8-2). To sharpen, the squeegee

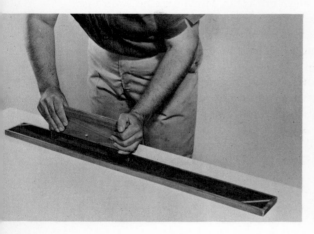

FIG. 8–2
Squeegee sharpener

is held vertically with the blade resting on the surface of the sandpaper and sharpened with even, light, lengthwise strokes. The pressure must be the same at both ends of the blade.

The sharpener illustrated in Fig. 8-3 is made with three strips of wood; a base strip to which the sandpaper is attached and two guide strips that aid in keeping the squeegee blade vertical during the sharpening stroke. A length of sandpaper about ¾ inch wide is placed down the center of the base strip. Shims of index or card stock, built up to the same thickness as the sandpaper, are abutted on both sides of the sandpaper strip. The guide strips are attached to overlap the sandpaper and are placed just far enough apart to allow the squeegee blade to slide easily between the inner faces of the strips. The guide strips may be nailed to the base strip, or may

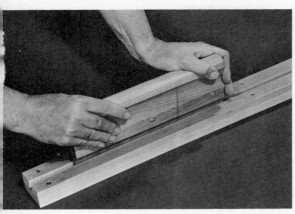

FIG. 8–3
Squeegee sharpener
with guide strips

be attached with screws for more convenient removal when the sandpaper needs to be changed.

The sharpener should be at least a foot longer than the longest squeegee to be sharpened so that the squeegee blade will not slide beyond the end of the sandpaper during the sharpening stroke. Crumbs of blade material removed by sanding should be wiped carefully from the blade before it is used.

SCREEN FABRIC. Even though the equipment was thoroughly cleaned after the previous printing, before each use check for dirt or grit that may have settled on the screen fabric.

REGISTER TABS. Keep register tabs in good condition. Replace worn tabs or tape that has become softened by solvents. Before removing old tabs, place a copy from the edition in registration and

135

tape it to the baseboard to serve as a guide for positioning new tabs. Install new tabs as outlined in "Register Tabs," Chapter 3, placing them in the same locations as the old tabs.

ALIGNMENT BLOCKS.   Check alignment blocks frequently and adjust them if space is visible between the blocks and the screen frame.

HINGE PINS.   Make sure the hinge pins are all the way in the hinges. If pins are lost, a nail which fits snugly will substitute.

ACCESSORIES.   Check the functioning of any mechanical accessories, such as the screen prop.

Repairs

TORN TAPE BARRIER.   The tape barrier that fills the inside corners between the screen fabric and the frame is usually the item requiring most frequent repair. Torn tape may allow color mixture to accumulate under the edge of the frame between the frame and the fabric. When hardened, this mixture may cut the fabric. Therefore, it is advisable to replace torn tape at once.

Strip off as much of the old tape as possible and clean the fabric and frame surfaces thoroughly. If necessary, use lacquer thinner, alcohol, or steel wool to remove any traces of oil or finish that would prevent new tape from sticking. Install new tape and refinish as outlined in "The Screen," Chapter 2.

DAMAGED SCREEN FABRIC.   An accidental tear or puncture in the screen fabric may be repaired if small and outside the printing area. Any break should be given immediate attention, since it will enlarge if not repaired. Paste patches of paper tape over the hole on both sides of the fabric and paint them with lacquer or shellac. A small puncture or broken thread can be kept from spreading with a dab of lacquer or shellac.

If the puncture falls within the printing area, it should be left untouched. As long as the damage remains slight, it will have little effect on printing, but if the hole grows so that its presence becomes evident in the print, the fabric must be changed.

To change the screen fabric, remove all the staples or tacks holding the fabric to the frame and peel off the old material. Tear off as much of the tape barrier from the frame as possible and clean and sand the bottom and inside edge of the frame down to a fresh wood surface. Install new fabric and tape barrier and refinish as outlined in "The Screen," Chapter 2.

WARPED SCREEN FRAME. A warped screen frame can be a nuisance during printing and may affect the quality of the printed surface. A warp caused by stress at the corners of the frame can sometimes be relieved by twisting the frame in the direction opposite the warp. An excessive amount of pressure applied in this way may loosen the corners, so proceed with caution.

A warp in the frame member itself can usually be straightened by weighting the member to bend it slightly in the opposite direction. Leave weights in place for several days, then check progress. If the warp persists, the finish can be removed, the wood soaked in water for several hours, and the weighting repeated until the wood is dry.

WARPED BASEBOARD. A warped baseboard can usually be straightened by framing with wood strips attached to the bottom. The strips should be at least 1 by 2 inches in size. Attach these to the baseboard by their narrow edge with screws installed from the top of the baseboard near the margins. If an attachment must be made under the printing area, countersink the screw below the surface of the baseboard. After tightening the screw, fill the hole with wood filler, sand flush with the surface, and refinish.

9
THE FINISHED PRINT

When the last stencil has been printed, the creative activity is finished, but the life of the print as an entity has just begun. What is to happen to it now? If the artist is a professional, his work must contribute to his sustenance. A considerable amount of time is directed to this end; inefficiency or irresponsibility in the business of printmaking can make deep inroads on the time available to make prints. This chapter describes the disposition of the print after it is completed: its identification, storage, and exhibition.

Identification

When the copies of the finished print are dry, the edition should be selected and each copy identified with copy and edition numbers,

Tavern by Hulda D. Robbins

title, artist's signature, and date. An *edition* in printmaking usually denotes all those copies of the print that are duplicates and represent the artist's decision of the best state of the print. Varied opinions are advanced on what constitutes a duplicate. Even with the best controls, minute variations will occur from copy to copy due to slight differences in printing action. If equipment is kept in good condition and reasonable controls are practiced in printing, these variations will be insignificant and of no consequence to the general visual import of the print.

Personal judgment controls the selection of prints for the edition. I use the following procedure: several copies are spread out at one time and carefully compared. Visual effects of the parts as well as of the total are checked. If one copy has a noticeable deviation from the others, it is set aside and replaced with a fresh copy. One or two copies at a time are replaced by new copies; duplicates are kept in a separate stack from those rejected. A skip, misregistration, or other printing fault on a copy will cause its rejection. An experienced and careful printer will not find a great number of rejects—probably less than ten per cent of his total copies, not including those used for proofing.

The stack of identical copies comprises the edition. The number of copies in the stack is the edition number. The copies are numbered consecutively. The copy number usually appears at the bottom margin just below the printed area and approximately centered left to right. The copy number is followed by a slash and then the total number of copies in the edition. For example, 5/40 would be placed on the fifth copy in an edition of 40. The assignment of copy numbers is arbitrary, since the order in which the copies are printed does not affect the serigraph in the same way as the intaglio or lithograph print, where the copies are numbered relative to their printed sequence. Some serigraphers do not use the copy number at all, but enter only the total number in the edition. However, I find the copy number handy for keeping records of the copies.

The rejects from the edition may receive other identification. This practice also varies among artists. I label all trial proofs as "studio proof," and, when progressive proofs have been kept of the individual stencils or stencil series, these copies are labeled as such. All other copies are designated as rejects, or destroyed.

Records

Since printmaking involves many more produced items than painting, sculpture, or most other fine art media, record keeping is more complex and more important to the printmaker. If he is an active exhibitor, he may have several copies from an edition scattered over the country at one time. Because he is working in a multicopy medium, he can distribute identical prints to several galleries. On occasion, he may need to recall prints for exhibition or sale, or revise prices, or borrow a copy from a patron. The easiest way to keep records of an inventory of prints is to start with the first edition and make the accounting a habit thereafter.

A biographical record maintained for every edition provides both a history and a current status report on each print. I use a ledger page for a comprehensive record of each edition, here recording the number of prints on hand, prices, purchases, loans, exhibitions, and awards. As well as this comprehensive record, two or three lines are reserved for each copy in the edition. Here notations will be made such as names and addresses of purchasers and whether the copy is framed or matted. Pages assigned to an edition may also contain other data such as the expenditure of time, technical information, and notes on materials used.

As well as the print inventory, a record of income from sales and awards and of all expenditures related to the making and disposition of the print should be carefully maintained. Any profit accrued from the sale of prints is subject to federal and sometimes state or local income taxes. All receipts or other records of legitimate expenses should be saved. Consultation with an accountant or tax adviser to determine items legally deductible as business expenses is worthwhile if the artist is serious about using his work as a source of income.

Print Storage and Handling

Proper print storage, necessary for the safety of the printed copies, also affords convenience when copies are removed to send to exhibitions, dealers, or to show to interested friends.

After identifying and recording the copies of a new edition, I remove several prints for a portfolio of copies "in use" and place the remainder in a folder for storage. The "in use" portfolio makes prints from all editions available in one location, to draw from upon demand. The bulk of the edition can be stored undisturbed except for occasional portfolio replenishment.

The storage folder must be durable and stiff enough to help support the edition stack during handling. Medium weight cardboard or chip board is satisfactory and does not use much storage space. The folder should be large enough to completely cover the stack. Identification by title on one corner makes the folder easier to locate when stacked with others in a storage unit.

Preferably folders should be stored flat. If stacked on edge, unless tightly compressed, the edition paper is likely to slump and become rippled. Rolled storage should also be avoided; no matter how well the roll is protected, it is always in danger of being crushed. In addition, having taken the set of the roll, a copy is very difficult to mat or frame. Rolling may also loosen the bond between the paint layers and the paper, causing the paint to check or flake off when flattened.

Because the serigraph often has a thicker paint deposit, it is more sensitive to some kinds of mishandling than prints in other media. Sharp creases in the printed area may cause the paint layers over the crease to crack and come loose from the paper. Scratches and abrasions create their share of print casualties. A scratch may be the result of curious probing with a fingernail or an accidental contact with a sharp object. Protection from these may warrant framing the print under glass.

Loss of prints due to careless practice during production and subsequent handling can shrink the edition. Accidental damage can be minimized by using common sense in locating and using studio equipment and by using sensible precautions in copy handling.

To prevent damage during production, keep the print drying racks out of traffic zones. Avoid strong drafts in the drying area that may whip the paper or blow it from the hangers. Check for malfunctioning or weak pins each time copies are hung to dry, and, when moving copies, as from the drying rack to the printing area, avoid any practice that might cause a print to be dropped.

To avoid excessive bending, support the print with both hands when handling a copy in a horizontal position. To free both hands in printing, use a prop to hold the screen frame up while inserting or removing copies. When moving a stack of prints, place a stiff cardboard underneath.

To prevent scratches and abrasion, do not slide a copy out from the middle of a stack; remove the top copies first. To remove loose grit or foreign particles from the surface of a print, use a soft brush such as a desk brush. Protect the face of the print with tissue, acetate, glass, or other appropriate material whenever it is packaged or displayed where it may be subject to accidental scratches or abrasion.

Matting and Framing

For temporary display, such as museum exhibitions or gallery portfolios, prints are most often matted. A mat should set the print off from distracting elements in the surroundings without itself being too obtrusive or prominent. For some special exhibitions or when a print is to be permanently displayed in a home, a frame adds an appropriate finish, provides the print with permanent protection, and serves as a transitional element between the print and its environment.

MATTING. A carefully made mat will enhance a good print as well as give it moderate protection. The term "mat" refers to the outside mask that borders the print and also is used to designate the assembly of the mat and attached backing board. Usually the mat is hinged to the backing board at the top edge and the print is positioned to the opening in the mat but fixed to the backing board. With this assembly, damaged or dirty mats can be replaced with fresh ones without disturbing the print copy.

Normally the mat opening will not fall at the edge of the print; a margin of about ¼ inch is left between the printed area and the edge of the mat opening at the top and sides; a slightly wider space is left at the bottom to accommodate the signature and identification. Conventionally, mats are cut wider at the bottom than at the sides and top. I feel this has little functional or esthetic value however, and prefer to cut my mats equally wide on all four sides. A three- or four-inch mat is usually sufficient for an average size print.

The standard material for the outside mask is pebble or smooth surfaced mat board. A variety is available in single or double weights, in several colors, and in many surface textures. The backing for the mat can be made from stock such as chip board, mounting board, or corrugated cardboard of about the same weight or thicker than the mat board. The backing should be sufficiently stiff to stand without slumping when resting in a near-vertical position. Because both mat and backing boards usually contain chemicals that may, in time, cause discoloration in the adjacent print copy, some print-makers isolate the copy with an intermediate layer of edition paper. Gummed paper tape of the type moistened with water is recommended for hinging. The same kind of tape or wheat paste is usually used for attaching the print to the backing.

The appearance of the mat—the care with which it was made and the condition in which it is shown—reflects on the artist's attitude toward his work. Cut mats with a razor-sharp knife to prevent ragged edges. Use a straightedge if necessary to insure a straight cut. Keep mats scrupulously clean and protect their corners from damage.

FRAMING. When the print is to be framed, my preference is for the simplest presentation which will protect the print and set off its visual statement. The color, molding section, and size of the frame and its liner are chosen with regard for the particular print and for its place of hanging, if this is permanent. The image may be bold, suggesting containment by a strong frame of substantial width and contrast. On the other hand, the image may suggest extension beyond its physical limits, or be more delicate in form and suggest a narrower and less contrasting frame. The permanent environment may have a strong influence on the scale and color of the framing material. If the print is to be hung on wood paneling, a similar color and finish may be appropriate to the frame. If the walls and furnishings have simple, clean design, the frame should reflect this. The frame in all cases should be sublimated to the printed image.

When the installation of the framed piece is unknown or is to be frequently changed, I prefer a molding of simple cross section, usually deeper than it is wide. Depth in the frame provides both structural and visual strength and allows the face of the print to project out from the wall, providing some visual isolation. The narrow front of the frame satisfies the concurrent need for a visual transition between the framed piece and its surroundings without overpowering the image. Inside this frame, a two- to three-inch border around the printed area further sets off the pictorial area of the print. While a liner of linen or mat board may be used, I prefer to frame the print unmatted, using the margins of the print as the border if these are clean and of adequate dimension.

The advisability of glassing the print depends upon the circumstances in which it will be hung. Except under the most carefully controlled light, glass will cause distracting reflections and make the print less easy to view. On the other hand, glass protects the print from dirt, curious probing, and other hazards. If the print is subject to these, I use glass.

When a print is to be framed without glass, the print should be adhered to a backing board to prevent warping and buckling of the paper with changes in temperature or humidity. Mounting a print is a delicate operation requiring care to avoid damage to the print and to assure complete, bubble-free adhesion. Several practice mountings with blank paper or proofs are recommended before attempting to mount a print for the first time.

No special equipment is required for mounting a print with glue. The glue must be mixed lump-free and the print handled carefully to avoid stretching or creasing the wet paper. A slow drying glue is necessary to allow time for the glue-covered paper to expand and for positioning the print on the backing. The glue must not stain or discolor the paper. Wheat paste and some of the newer plastic-based pastes designed for adhering wall paper have these characteristics. Rubber cement is not suitable for permanent mounting. The backing board must be a stiff, warp-free material with a smooth surface which will not be raised by the wet glue. Untempered hardboard is excellent.

The glue is applied with a soft bristle brush, first on the back of the print so the paper can expand while the backing board is being covered with glue. Position the print carefully over the board and gently smooth the paper onto the board, then cover the face of the print with clean wrapping paper and roll the print down thoroughly with a brayer, working outward from the center.

A light spraying with a plastic spray, such as the fixatives or clear plastic sprays sold in pressure cans, will make the print surface easier to clean. If several very light coats are used, some protection may be gained without a significant color change and the surface will remain relatively nonreflective.

Exhibiting

In exhibiting, the printmaker has a dual purpose of publicly introducing and marketing his graphic ideas. Public and private exhibitions offer many opportunities. Nearly every community holds regular exhibitions which are well attended and reviewed by critics. These exhibitions provide a forum for the artist's viewpoints, as he gives others an opportunity to see and to respond to his work.

Most exhibitions require submitted work to attain certain standards in order to be shown. Standards are based on the personal judgment of the selection committee; any competitive exhibition will necessarily impose the opinion of the jury on the work of the artist. Invitational exhibitions are also "juried" in the sense that the artists invited are selected by the sponsors.

Competitive exhibitions are juried by one person or a small group of jurors chosen by the sponsors or organizers of the exhibition. The jurors may be printmakers or other artists, museum directors, curators, or critics who accept for showing what they believe to be the best of the work submitted, and select outstanding pieces for awards, purchase prizes, and honorable mentions. A major exhibition may include only a small fraction of the entries submitted, which sometimes number several thousand.

The bulk of print exhibitions held in public museums, galleries, or fairs are competitions open to all artists within a specified area; an *international* show is open to all artists in all or in several specified countries; a *national* is open to all artists in this country; a *regional*, to artists in one or several specified states; and a *local* may include only those artists in one or a few counties, or may be further limited to a district or community.

Many printmaking groups, schools, and galleries hold regular exhibitions at a regional or local level. These competitions may be as highly selective as a major national exhibition because of more limited gallery space. Regional or local exhibitions often combine prints and drawings; watercolors may also be included, and exhibitions open to all media are not unusual.

A listing of exhibition opportunities may be found in most art magazines or posted at museums, galleries, and art schools. Announcements usually appear well in advance of the exhibition explaining where to inquire for details. A prospectus will be sent upon request, telling what entries are eligible, how they should be prepared for display, when and where they should be submitted, the amount of the entry fee, the prizes to be awarded, and the names of jury members. Entry forms and labels will also be furnished.

The primary purpose of an exhibition at a public institution is the showing, rather than the selling, of art; greater sales potential is available through private galleries and agents. Some private galleries have attained a stature that gives their exhibitions much the same prominence as those at major museums.

The artist may be invited to show his work at a gallery, if he has an established reputation, or he may apply to a gallery for representation. Galleries take work on consignment and charge a percentage of the price when the work is sold, usually 30 to 40 per cent of the sales price. A contract should be drawn that states the terms of the consignment and other agreements such as exclusive territory rights, payment periods, time limitations either party may wish to set, methods of display, and reproduction rights. When prints are delivered to the gallery a listing in duplicate should be provided by the artist naming each print with copy number, medium, and retail price (which should be noted as including gallery commission). The duplicate listing should be signed by the gallery representative and retained by the artist as a receipt.

A good gallery relationship can be an important asset to the artist. The gallery may be his major spokesman; through the gallery his work may contact its greatest public. Many galleries are small in size but large in their devotion to art—few find the task a lucrative one.

An agent is usually a salesman who sells work to individual buyers. He will probably represent many artists, as a gallery does, but takes his portfolios directly to the potential customers, often interior decorators, specialty shops, schools, or libraries. The chances of selling more pieces, perhaps whole editions, are often greater with an agent than with a gallery, but the return per piece is usually less;

often the artist will receive only one-fourth to one-half the sales price. However, if this price is a lump sum offered as a commission for an edition, it may be quite attractive.

Packaging the Print for Shipment

The exhibiting printmaker has an advantage over the painter and sculptor in the relative ease with which his work can be prepared for submittal and shipped to an exhibition. Only rarely is framing required; prints are traditionally exhibited in mats and thus may be shipped in easily constructed, lightweight, inexpensive packages.

Before packaging, make sure the print is properly identified, numbered, and signed. Check the entry form carefully to see that information requested is complete and attach labels firmly in the proper locations.

A well constructed package not only protects the print during shipment, but can be timesaving for the exhibition staff when they unpack and repack the entry. For matted prints, a lightweight package that provides adequate protection can be made with two pieces of heavy corrugated cardboard cut slightly larger than the matted dimension of the largest print to be shipped. The prints are sandwiched between the pieces of cardboard. The edges of thin packages may be sealed with gummed paper tape; thicker packages should be taped under compression and enclosed in heavy wrapping paper. Tape all seams and label the package with destination, return address, and special handling instructions.

If so specified in the exhibition prospectus, the print may be shipped unmatted and rolled in a mailing tube. Rolling to not less than a four-inch diameter will not damage a serigraph if care is taken that the roll can be withdrawn from the tube without damage. Cover the print surface with tissue and roll the print, face out, so it will fit snugly but not tightly in the tube. Tape to prevent unrolling and insert in the tube. Close the ends of the tube securely.

Ship entries so they will arrive at their destination shortly before the due date; too early arrivals may cause storage problems for the exhibition sponsors. The method of shipment will depend upon time, facilities, and distances involved. Consult local agencies such as the Post Office and express firms for their special requirements for packaging, insurance, pickup, and delivery.

Danish Terrain
by Judy Hanshue

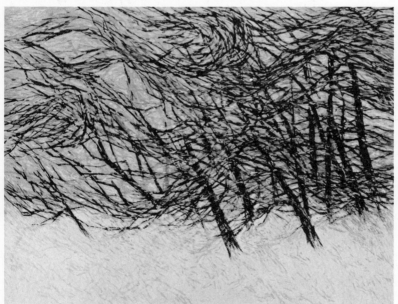

Gale by Harold Booth

APPENDIX

Pigment Compounds

Serigraphy is not troubled with a shortage of adaptable color materials. A dazzling assortment of hues in several pigment compounds is available for the artist's choosing. Such an abundance doesn't simplify the selection of the most appropriate materials, however. Compounds of pigments and some of their necessary qualities for serigraphy are discussed below to aid in the selection of a palette of colors. Methods for evaluating pigment compounds are described and a palette of tested colors is suggested.

Color Materials for Serigraphy

The color materials most frequently used in serigraphy are screen process colors, tinting colors or toners, artist's oils, base ink pigments, and processed printing inks. These materials are compounded by suspending pigments, finely ground colored substances,

Sun Caught in Rock by Sylvia Wald

in vehicles composed of materials such as oils, varnishes, dryers, stabilizers, and extenders. The pigment material, the composition of the vehicle, and the proportion of pigment to vehicle will depend upon the use for which the color material was designed and will affect the permanency, tinting strength, transparency, drying time, flexibility, and other qualities of the color material.

Thus, many factors are important in selecting a palette besides hue. Permanency is a major concern—there are few artists who wish to witness their colors slowly disappear while the print is on display. Not all color materials are equally permanent; many excellent hues will fade or darken when exposed to light. Fortunately, a good hue range is available in materials which are permanent.

High tinting strength and transparency are also critical factors when the pigment compound is to be extended for transparent or semi-transparent printing. The balance of tinting strength and transparency in a color material controls the relative intensity that is possible for a particular degree of transparency. In other words, the balance controls the ability of a color mixture to cover or dominate underlying colors at a particular intensity. For example, Hansa and benzadine yellow are two bright yellows, both of high tinting strength but much different in transparency. A mixture of one part benzadine yellow with ten parts extender would produce a more transparent layer of yellow than an equivalent proportion of Hansa and extender; to equal the transparency of the benzadine yellow mixture, about three times as much base would have to be added to the Hansa yellow, resulting in a great drop in intensity. Tinting strength and transparency require more attention in silk screen where color is applied in thin, even layers than in other media, such as oil painting, in which these factors can be manipulated to a greater extent by varying the paint thickness.

No one type of pigment compound is ideal for all types of printing; a greater number of desirable hues of high tinting strength and transparency range can be obtained by selecting from several sources. The prepared pigment compounds may also be modified by the serigrapher in his color mixture to control other qualities such as build and reflectivity. To achieve the desired range of hue, transparency, and surface character, he may draw from several of the materials described below.

Screen process colors are distributed in cans, usually quarts or gallons, and may be used directly as supplied for opaque color. Mixed with extender, screen process colors are also suitable for semi-transparent printing. However, the compound is valuable principally for its ability to cover almost any hue or contrast in one coat, and for its high build. Screen process colors may be acquired from screen supply houses and many art stores.

Tinting colors or *toners* contain a higher percentage of pigment than screen process colors. Some tinting colors are distributed especially for use in screen printing, others are intended for coloring other paints as well. The concentration of pigment in one brand of tinting colors may vary considerably from another brand, but all must be extended with a base mixture for use in screen printing. Tinting colors are often available in standard artist's hues. Screen supply houses and some art and paint stores carry one or two brands of tinting colors.

Artist's oils contain high concentrations of pigment and some of the stronger colors are especially suitable for semi-transparent and transparent mixtures. Artist's oils are the most expensive of all the pigment compounds, averaging two to three times the cost of other compounds using the same pigments. However, pigments of desirable hue and permanency not otherwise available may be found in artist's oils. Art stores and some stationery and paint stores carry several brands. Select the top grade of a particular brand.

Base ink pigments are the raw pigment pastes used by ink companies for formulating commercial printing inks. Pigment is ground more finely for inks than for oil paints; a base ink pigment will have the maximum amount of finely ground pigment in proportion to the grinding vehicle. Such pigments are ideal for transparent printing where they will retain good coloring strength even when dispersed in extender in proportions of 1 to 100 or more. Base inks are usually available only from ink companies. Not all companies will be interested in filling an order from their raw material; even if they are, they may require a purchase of a pound or more of each pigment. However, colors are available in base inks that may make the extra trouble to obtain them worthwhile. In addition to their usefulness in transparent screen printing, many of the pigments are excellent glazing colors for oil painting.

Processed printing inks are those prepared for commercial presses or for printmakers' use in lithography, intaglio, or relief printing. Varnishes and dryers are added to base inks, and some prepared colors may be mixtures of several pigments. As a group, commercial printing inks are generally unreliable in permanency and should be tested as described below. The nomenclature for these colors is also often misleading; for example, a mixture may be called by an earth-pigment name when no actual earth pigment is included. Natural earth pigments are too abrasive for use on commercial printing presses; earth colors are simulated with mixtures of other pigments. However, these inks are compounded of very high tinting strength pigments and may be greatly extended for transparent mixtures. Processed inks are available at houses that sell commercial printing supplies and printmaking inks may be found at some art stores.

Testing for Permanency, Tinting Strength, and Transparency

If a pigment is not a commonly used, traditional artist's color that has been thoroughly tested, its permanency may be questioned. Books on artist's materials may have evaluations of pigments that are infrequently used in artist's oils but that are more commonly used in other pigment compounds. Pigment manufacturers and ink processing companies may have permanency ratings for the pigments they make or use and will usually supply this information upon request. Ratings of processed inks, screen process colors, and tinting colors are sometimes supplied with catalogs and color sample cards, but keep in mind that these colors may be designed for printing applications where permanency is not a concern. Sometimes there is no real way to determine permanency except to test the color.

When the permanency of a desirable hue is in doubt, a simple exposure test is advisable. The easiest method is to screen a small area of the pigment on edition stock, using the same extender as for printing. Cut the sample in two parts and tape one part to the inside of a window that receives a great deal of sunlight. Keep the other part unexposed in a notebook, between the pages of a bound book, or in a dark shelf in the studio. The two parts may be compared at intervals; an impermanent pigment will start to change within days and may disappear within a month. I consider a six-month exposure to maximum sunlight with no or very slight fading or darkening as excellent or very good permanency. Such color will not change in many years of normal room illumination.

A slightly more elaborate test will supply additional information on the tinting strength and transparency of a pigment. In this test a measured proportion of pigment and extender may be screened on a test card in which part of the printing area has been preprinted with small areas of primary colors and black. Several samples of the pigment mixed with varying proportions of extender should be printed. In such a test I have printed base inks, processed inks, and artist's oils in proportions of 1 part pigment to 12, 25, 50, and 100 parts extender mixture; screen process colors were used as supplied and diluted with 1, 3, 7, and 15 parts extender; and tinting colors with up to 30 parts extender, or to 60 parts for one especially potent brand.

Relative tinting strength and transparency can be gauged by comparing the set of cards for one pigment with the cards of another pigment. Tinting strength will be indicated by the relative rate the pigment loses intensity as more extender is added; this is the reason for the sequence of cards for each pigment—a high tinting strength transparent pigment may visually appear weaker when printed, due to its greater passage of light, than a moderate strength opaque pigment which can better cover over undercolors or the white of the printing stock. Nonetheless the high tinting strength pigment will lose less intensity when greatly extended. Transparency is indicated on the test cards by the amount the pigment dominates or blocks the preprinted colors on the card.

Recommended Palette of Colors

This compilation is selected from about one hundred pigments that I have tested and used for printing. Except as noted the permanency of each is excellent or very good. Other pigments could certainly be included in this list—I have attempted to choose primarily those pigments that would provide a satisfactory hue range, that are high in tinting strength, or that have other desirable qualities as described.

All the pigments listed are distributed by their name in either artist's oils or base inks. Some brands of tinting colors and some processed printing inks and screen process colors use the pigment name, but many colors have titles such as brown, magenta, fire red, etc., that do not identify their pigment. If the manufacturer or processor is not willing to disclose the pigments used in such a compound, it should be tested. The frequent use of this type of color designations in many brands has made it impractical to compile a more comprehensive list here.

Blue   Phythalocyanine blue
       Milori blue
       Ultramarine blue

In base inks, phythalocyanine blue may be available in a blue-red or blue-green cast, but one is not significantly different from the other. Phythalocyanine blues are transparent and high in tinting strength. Milori blue is an extremely powerful pigment of more greenish character than the phythalocyanine blue and slightly more opaque. Ultramarine is a warm blue, has moderate tinting strength, and is semi-transparent.

Green   Phythalocyanine green
       Chromium oxide green

Phythalocyanine green is available in the familiar bluish cast or, in inks called Q. S. Cyan, with a yellow-green cast. These colors are transparent and high in tinting strength. Chromium oxide is an earthy opaque green of high tinting strength.

Yellow   Hansa yellow
       Iron or Mars yellow
       Raw umber
       Burnt umber
       Benzadine yellow

Hansa is a bright yellow of high tinting strength. Iron, or Mars, yellow is similar in hue to yellow ochre. Raw and burnt umber are earthy browns. All of the above yellow pigments are opaque and have high tinting strength.

Benzadine yellow has only good permanency, tending to fade slightly with exposure, but is included here because it is very transparent, has high tinting strength, and is an intense bright yellow.

Some of the bright yellows, such as primrose and lemon yellow, darken prominently with exposure. Pigments such as these are frequently used in screen process colors and printing inks; all bright yellows in these compounds should be tested if the label does not identify the pigment.

Orange   Rex orange
Cadmium orange

Rex orange darkens very slightly with exposure but can be rated as having very good permanency. It is a brilliant opaque orange of very high tinting strength, somewhat redder than cadmium. Cadmium orange has moderate tinting strength and is opaque.

Red   Phythalocyanine scarlet
Cadmium red
Super Jac Lake
Indian red
Burnt sienna

Phythalocyanine scarlet is unique among the reds in that it is the only fully permanent transparent red available in the bright reds. It is a fiery red, although slightly cooler than cadmium, with very good tinting strength. It is a relatively new and expensive pigment and may not be readily available except from an ink company. Cadmium red is moderate in tinting strength and opaque. Super Jac Lake is a transparent cool red, much like alizarin, but with higher tinting strength. Indian red is a cool, opaque, earthy red; and burnt sienna is a warm, semi-transparent earth red. Both Indian red and burnt sienna have high tinting strength.

Many other red pigments are available but as a group they are notorious for fading. A true bright red that has both permanency and high tinting strength is next to impossible to find. Unfortunately many attractive but impermanent red pigments are used in printing inks, screen process colors, tinting colors, and even one highly advertised artist's oil color that I have tested. Some of these reds will fade within a few days exposure to sunlight, and within a few weeks indoors at normal room lighting.

Purple   Mars violet
Manganese violet
Cerise toner

Mars violet is a distinctive, earthy color, not far removed from Indian red, but much cooler. Mars violet has very high tinting strength and opacity. Manganese violet is a fresh bright purple, transparent and moderate in tinting strength. Cerise toner is a brilliant red-purple of very high tinting strength, transparent, but has only good permanency.

Black Lamp black
  Job black

Most blacks have reliable permanency and the choice may depend on the tinting strength and build properties. Lamp black in artist's oils has much higher tinting strength than ivory black and is similar to job black, a name utilized in the printing inks. Screen process black may be chosen for its high build property and is also suitable for mixing with extender and other colors.

White Screen process white

The white sold as a screen process color provides more covering power for its cost than any combination of white pigment and extender that I have discovered. Screen process white will almost cover any undercolor fully in one coat or may be mixed with extender for semi-transparent layers.

BIBLIOGRAPHY

Biegeleisen, J. I., and Cohn, Max Arthur. *Silk Screen Techniques.* New York: Dover Publications, Inc., 1958.

Cahn, Joshua Binion, ed. *What is an Original Print?* New York: Print Council of America, 1964.

Heller, Jules. *Printmaking Today.* New York: Holt, Rinehart & Winston, Inc., 1958.

Mayer, Ralph. *The Artist's Handbook.* New York: The Viking Press, Inc., Revised Edition, 1957.

Shokler, Harry. *Artists Manual for Silk Screen Print Making.* New York: Tudor Publishing Co., 1960.

Stephenson, Jessie B. *From Old Stencils to Silk Screening: A Practical Guide.* New York: Charles Scribner's Sons, 1953.

INDEX

INDEX